THE OFFICIAL Rangers FANS' GUIDE

THIS IS A CARLTON BOOK

This edition produced for
The Book People Ltd,
Hall Wood Avenue,
Haydock,
St Helens WA11 9UL

10 9 8 7 6 5 4 3 2 1

Text and design copyright © Carlton Books Limited 1997

The club crest is a registered trademark of the Glasgow Rangers Football Club PLC.

All rights reserved. No part of this publication may be reproduced, stored in a retrieval system, or transmitted in any form or by any means, electronic, mechanical, photocopying, recording or otherwise, without the prior permission of the copyright owner and the publishers.

A CIP catalogue record for this book is available from the British Library

ISBN 1 85613 455 5

Project Editor: Martin Corteel
Project art direction: Paul Messam
Production: Garry Lewis and Sarah Schuman
Picture research: Victoria Walker
Designed by Michael Spender

Author's Acknowledgements:
Without the support and tolerance of the two women in my life, the Dandy L and the Dandy C, this book would not exist.
Thanks are also due to the following: The *Scottish Daily Mail*, *Rangers News*, R McElroy, Roberto Manservisi, J McNeish, A Capaldi, F Scimone.

Printed in Italy

The publishers would like to thank the following sources for their kind permission to reproduce the pictures in this book:

Allsport UK Ltd./Shaun Botterill, Simon Bruty, David Cannon, Russell Cheyne, Chris Cole, Trevor Jones, Ross Kinnaird, Steve Morton, Mark Pain, Ben Radford, Mark Thompson; Colorsport; Empics/Matthew Ashton, Phil O'Brien, Neal Simpson; Herald Evening Times, Glasgow/David Hare; London Features International/UFB; MSI; Popperfoto; Professional Sport; Scottish News and Sport; Sporting Pictures (UK) Ltd.; Topham Picture Point.

Every effort has been made to acknowledge correctly and contact the source and/copyright holder of each picture, and Carlton Books Limited apologises for any unintentional errors or omissions which will be corrected in future editions of this book.

THE OFFICIAL Rangers

FANS' GUIDE

THE STORY OF THE NINE-IN-A-ROW YEARS

GRAHAM HUNTER

TED SMART

Contents

Danish international Brian Laudrup is an Ibrox idol

Another Championship for a delighted Walter Smith

The magnificent Ibrox stadium from the outside

Introduction 7

Chapter 1
The History of Rangers 8
Traces the history of Rangers from the formation of the club in 1873 to the arrival of Graeme Souness in 1986; also includes profiles of all-time Rangers greats such as Alan Morton and Jim Baxter.

Chapter 2
The " Nine-in-a-row" Years 14
Describes the milestones of each of the "Nine-in-a-row" seasons starting with 1988–89 and finishing with the Brian Laudrup goal against Dundee United that clinched title number nine.

Chapter 3
Rangers in Europe 34
Examines Rangers' experiences in Europe down the years.

Chapter 4
Up for the Cup 44
Reviews the great tradition of Rangers in the Scottish and League Cups.

Chapter 5

"Nine-in-a-row" Stars 54

Profiles of the players who have graced the Ibrox turf during the "Nine-in-a-row" years; from Davie Cooper to Ally McCoist, all the greats are included.

Chapter 6

The Managers 70

Pays tribute to the managers who have helped maintain Rangers' magnificent traditions.

Chapter 7

Rangers' Foreign Stars 78

Profiles the foreign legion who have helped give Rangers a more cosmopolitan feel during the "Nine-in-a-row" years; includes Pieter Huistra and Jorg Albertz.

Chapter 8

The Stars of the Future 86

Looks into the club's crystal ball and profiles the Rangers' stars of tomorrow.

Chapter 9

The "Old Firm" Matches 92

Recounts the long and passionate history of probably the fiercest rivalry in world football – Rangers and Celtic

Chapter 10

At Home 102

Celebrates Ibrox, home of Rangers, and one of the most famous stadiums in Britain.

Chapter 11

The Other Great Matches 108

Detailed descriptions of some of the great matches involving Rangers during the "Nine-in-a-row" years

Chapter 12

The Records 114

Season-by-season statistics from 1988–89 to 1996–97, plus miscellaneous club records.

Index 128

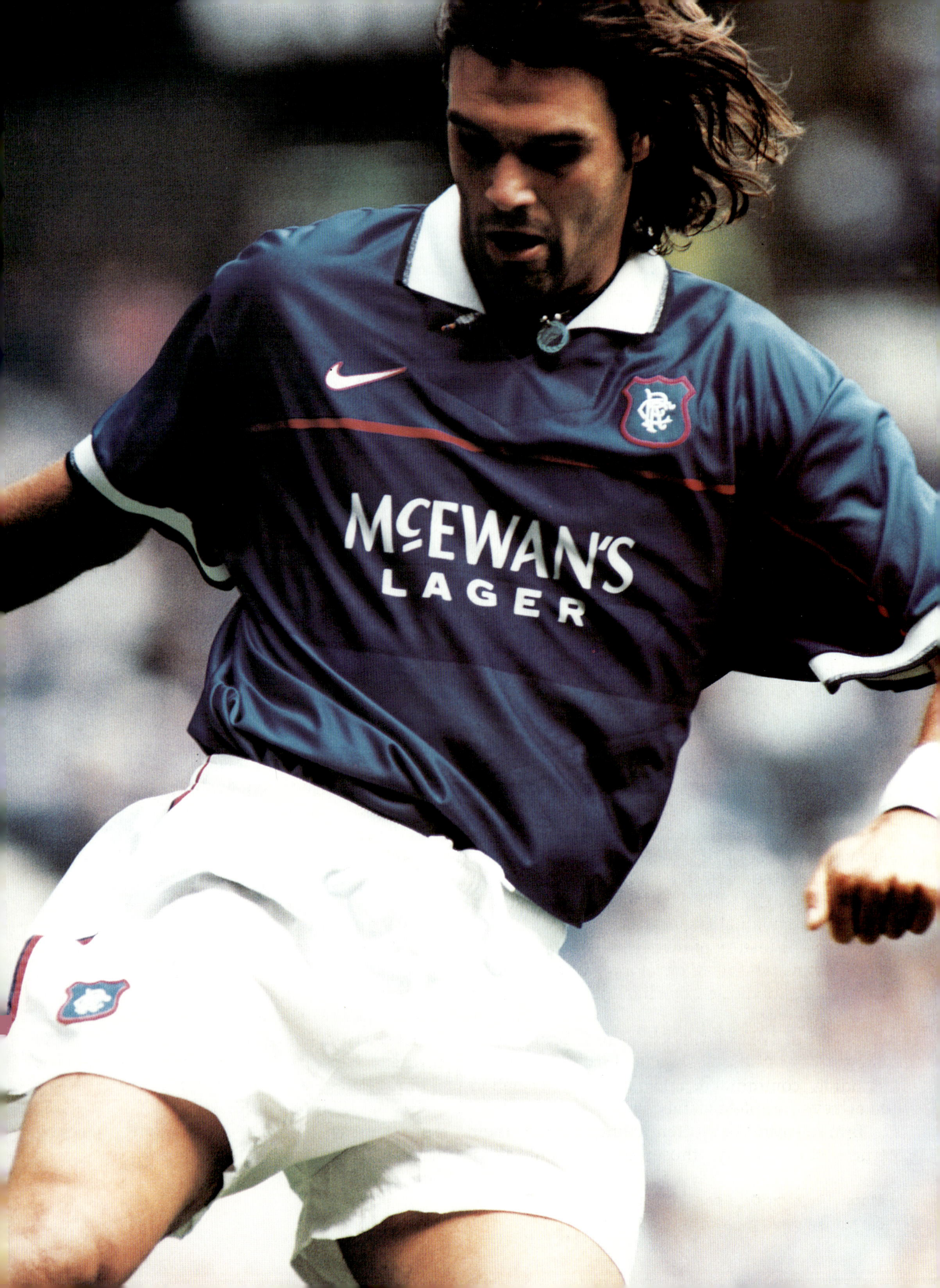

McEWAN'S
LAGER

Introduction

Rangers Football Club means many things to many different people all around the world, but there is no doubt that it is one of the clubs which, across its history, has helped to make football great. Triumph and tragedy have woven their strands together throughout the 124 years during which Rangers have incorporated some of the most colourful men ever to participate in the sport into their own story.

Such is its impact on its own environs and beyond, with each generation of Scots which pursues fame and fortune around the globe, that this is more than a mere football organisation which is just the product of points, trophies and players. It is an institution whose growth has mirrored the social and industrial developments in its home city, Glasgow, and in its mother country, Scotland.

With fledgling roots in 1872 and foundation a year later Rangers were born during a time when football was a new and blooming phenomenon in Scotland as well as Great Britain as a whole: a phenomenon so immense it could be compared to that of computers, technology and the Internet now.

Everyone wanted to play football as clubs sprang up all over the country, but Rangers were indubitably the first truly big Scottish club, 15 years before Celtic and quickly overtaking the originally redoubtable Queen's Park.

Theirs is a history of managers, directors, players and fans who have developed a deep love of the club and dedicated much of their working life to its betterment.

Bill Struth, Willie Waddell, George Young, John Greig, Jock Wallace, David Murray – men of standing, commitment and fierce determination to achieve complete victory.

But, despite too often being denied their true character by those who resent their dominance, Rangers have also given the game of football some of its most wonderfully entertaining characters.

Alan Morton and Jim Baxter are spoken of with reverence today because their talent dwarfed that of most players in the modern game: were they up for transfer in the current market, the price would set new and even more jaw-dropping levels.

Willie Henderson, Ally McCoist, Bob McPhail, Willie Woodburn and Willie Johnston: Rangers have had players to fire the blood and send adrenalin pumping through the veins of their fans since before the beginning of this century.

Now they are in an era where they are no longer tied to the industrial and social trends of their home and, under the visionary leadership of David Murray, have cut loose in order to become a massive industry in their own right – one which is hungry to take its place at the table when a new European order is formed over the next few years. Nine-in-a-row has been achieved and there will inevitably be more domestic highs to follow, but Rangers are embarking on the build-up to a new century with a determination to build a squad which can compete with the elite and entertain its devoted followers by emulating that solitary, glorious European trophy win in 1972.

The new journey will be no less dramatic than the last 124 years, and could be even more triumphant.

Marco Negri made a sensational start to his Rangers' career with five goals against Dundee Utd

Chapter 1
The History of Rangers

It seems inconceivable, now that Rangers are a worldwide phenomenon, one of Britain's wealthiest clubs and the most successful in Scottish football history, that they were formed on nothing more than the whim of a group of young students in 1872.

In a time when football was all the rage and clubs were being born at the rate rabbits breed, before quickly disappearing, they could easily have hit hard times and disbanded. In the first four years of their existence they played only three clubs which still remain today, Queen's Park, Partick and Dumbarton, while countless others of that era simply vanished. Many of them were stronger than Rangers at one stage or another but the club was held rock-steady by three families – the Vallances, the McNeils and the Campbells – across their initial seasons. Although long dead, these enthusiastic amateurs are owed so much by everyone for whom Rangers are a life-passion today.

Rangers quickly became one of the bastions of the game in Scotland, especially compared with more remote clubs. The *Scottish Athletic Journal* of 15 September 1882 reported of their Cup tie against Jordanhill: "The Rangers were highly amused on their arrival at the outlying village to see the preparations...the field was a new one and anything but a bowling green and no touchline had been marked. But Jordanhill quickly discovered a remedy and, borrowing a horse and plough from a neighbouring farmer, turned up a furrow and formed the necessary parallelogram with it. The furrow, however, was very dangerous, some of the Rangers getting nasty wrenches."

It is Moses McNeil who is believed to have chosen the name "Rangers" after a touring English rugby side whose name he liked. Meanwhile Celtic, whose name is inextricably linked with that of "The Rangers", did not exist until 16 years after Callendar and Rangers fought out a 0–0 draw on Glasgow Green – the club's first recorded match. During that time, they were rather quaintly true to Moses McNeil's choice of name, ranging far across Britain to play Oxford, Nottingham, Sheffield, Blackburn and Aston Villa.

Just as today, David Murray, and Walter Smith would be quite happy to accept the regular victories Rangers then recorded in England, it is fascinating to note that the currently-fashionable topic of the Ibrox giants playing in a better standard of league, in England, is old hat. For example, Rangers actually made it to the semi-final of the FA Cup in 1886–87 by beating Everton, Church, Cowlairs, Lincoln City and Old Westminsters before losing 3–1 to Aston Villa.

The year of Celtic's formation, 1888, brought the first Old Firm match (although it took years for the two teams to acquire that nickname) when Rangers

In the flying winger Alan Morton, Rangers had one of Scotland's few footballing geniuses

lost 5–2 to a scratch Celtic side culled from clubs throughout the district. It is reported that both sides retired for joint revelries after the match, in a completely friendly atmosphere, something which would become a touch unusual in later years.

Ibrox Stadium, like any grand old dame who has looked out over such great sadness and joy in 125 years, has undergone a few facelifts in her time. She was brought kicking and screaming into this world on 20 August 1887, when almost 20,000 people watched Preston North End win 8–1.

The penultimate day of the century brought Rangers to a new, larger ground on a nearby site which, in a dreadful foretaste of events many years later, was to prove a tragic one. And by 1900, Old Firm fever had put its vice-like grip round Glasgow's neck: 60,000 fans in a week watched two Rangers vs. Celtic cup matches, with the Gers winning by the odd goal in 13.

The new stadium might have been a landmark, but 26 people died there during the 1902 Scotland vs. England international, when part of the West Terracing collapsed just as thousands leaned forward to watch winger Bobby Templeton surge past the England defenders.

The early years of the 20th century went largely – although by no means exclusively – to the other half of the Old Firm. Yet it was not until the postwar social changes in Ireland started to have an effect on Glasgow, the massive industrial magnet, that the entrenchment which has brought much of the bitterness between supporters really set in.

Celtic had been founded for the good of the Catholic poor of the East End, while Rangers simply had a footballing basis, but immigrant Irish Protestants naturally flocked to the "other", non-Catholic club. By the 1920s, names started to emerge which still remain legendary, even to today's teenage supporters of the club.

Alan MORTON

In the great training ground in the sky, Alan Morton will have been looking down approvingly on Brian Laudrup these last few seasons, because the Dane is a true inheritor of the Wee Blue Devil's scintillating skills. During an era of flamboyant, hard-drinking showmen Morton was, by comparison, every inch the professional but could better any one of his contemporaries on the pitch. Bill Struth's first signing for the club, in 1920, he is still a Rangers legend, but many of his most extraordinary games were for Scotland. Three goals in the Wembley Wizards match of 1928, when Scotland beat England 5–1, came from his crosses; and his Rangers colleague, Tommy Cairns, compared him with Stanley Matthews, saying: "In the other arts, accuracy of the pass and cross, dribbling and team sense, he was Matthews's equal. In directness and goalscoring Morton was better." Five feet four inches tall, Morton was a natural right-footer but practised as a boy in Airdrie until his left became an unstoppable weapon. The Wee Blue Devil, as English journalist Ivan Sharpe christened him, retired in the 1932–33 season after 495 games and 115 goals, becoming a Rangers director until 1968. He died, a year before Rangers' great European triumph, in 1971.

Few trophies have felt as sweet to win for Rangers as the 1928 Scottish Cup – after a 25 year wait

Bob McPhail, whose scoring record Ally McCoist has only recently overtaken, was signed from Airdrie and Alan Morton became one of Scotland's greatest wingers – The Wee Blue Devil. But perhaps the most significant was Bill Struth, their legendary manager who somehow stamped his personality on the club in a way which has never been fundamentally changed. It wasn't just because he spent 34 years in charge: it was because Struth believed that Rangers should be the best, that second was nowhere and that nothing and nobody was to get in the way.

Struth had a passionate belief in physical fitness and had joined the club as a trainer, only succeeding Willie Wilton, the first manager, when he tragically drowned after falling from a friend's yacht. Struth, to judge by every account of the time, took pride in teaching all his employees to parade their superiority: in their dress, their use of first-class travel, and even in an arrogant attitude to life. Like a great Chinese mandarin, he cared little about what actually made the kingdom work as long as the workers were working to his satisfaction and his word was law. Struth barely interfered in footballing matters, leaving them to *ad hoc* committees of senior players which dictated team selection and tactics.

Rangers celebrated their 50th anniversary in 1922–23 in style, by embarking on a run of 17 seasons lasting up until the outbreak of the Second World War, during which the club won the Championship 13 times. Also, in 1928, having not won the Scottish Cup for a quarter of a century, they defeated Celtic 4–0 in the final and went on to win it repeatedly. When war again arrived the Southern League was instituted, and Rangers took it on seven consecutive occasions.

But no matter how dominant the Gers have become throughout their long, proud history, there has always been ebb and flow. Post-war, Rangers were strong, but there were changes coming and Hibernian's Famous Five of Gordon Smith, Bobby Johnstone, Lawrie Reilly, Eddie Turnbull and Willie Ormond took Leagues in 1948, 1951 and 1952, scoring 1,500 goals between them during their heyday.

Still, this is an era remembered for the defensive "Iron Curtain", personified by Bobby Brown, George Young and Willie Woodburn but also including Jock "Tiger" Shaw, Sammy Cox and Ian McColl.

George YOUNG

George "Corky" Young was Rangers' dominant figure during the middle part of the century. A giant of a man in physical stature, influence on the club and personality, those who didn't see Corky play can gain some understanding merely by looking at the pictures of him leading Rangers or Scotland out as captain and comparing him to the normal-sized opposition captains he absolutely dwarfs. He was part of the famous Iron Curtain defence in the 1940s and 1950s which happened to comprise defensive experts such as Willie Woodburn, Jock Shaw and Bobby Brown. Young's mammoth punts out of defence became part of Rangers' fairly simple counter-attack theory, but the Iron Curtain conceded only 180 goals in 180 games over six seasons. Captain of Scotland 48 times, he also led his country to consecutive victories against England at Wembley – 3–1 in 1949 and 3–2 in 1951. Under Bill Struth, Young was largely in control of team matters, selection, tactics, training and so on, and can therefore claim some credit for the 12 Championship, Cup and League Cup victories Rangers collected during his 428 games. Christened Corky for the champagne cork he carried everywhere with him, this was a man who lived life with vigour. George died in 1996.

In the decade from 1946 to 1956, Rangers won 22 trophies and the team's defence became legendary. These were still the days when anything up to 143,000 people, an incredible total, would watch a single match and Scotland still led the world in terms of attendances. Rangers were in the vanguard of those clubs which could attract a crowd the size of a city to watch them play.

George Young was a colossal figure on the pitch

The Iron Curtain was pulled apart in spectacular fashion when the Referee Committee of the Scottish Football Association suspended Willie Woodburn indefinitely, or *sine die*, for a long record of hot temper, strongly-articulated rebukes to referees and violent conduct. The *sine die* ban was lifted in 1957.

Already it was a transitional time, with Bill Struth's health failing and Scot Symon assuming control. The game was becoming more demanding, with changes in style emanating from Spain, Hungary and Italy soon to threaten the British belief that, as originators of the game, they ought to reign supreme.

Perhaps Rangers were not short-sighted regarding these changes, but simply focused on longer-term matters, as John Lawrence assumed control of the Ibrox board and set about revitalizing the club's financial base until it was probably the most affluent in Britain. In fact by 1963, Symon was in Spain to study the methods of that magnificent Real Madrid team. Symon, the new coach, was hampered by the immediate loss of Woodburn and Sammy Cox, while George Young went the following year.

Rangers did not win the Cup between 1953 and 1960, but the Championship was still regularly theirs and that was enough. More to the point, Rangers lost only four of their 24 League matches with Celtic in the 12 years of Symon's reign – not all that the directors required, but more than enough for the fans, who reigned supreme on the Saturday night after yet another Old Firm win.

Symon's legacy was the creation of a marvellous Rangers squad – Greig, Baxter, Brand, Henderson, Johnston, McLean – but Jock Stein had begun to weave his spell across the city and despite two European finals in the Sixties, a treble in 1964 and numerous other trophies, Symon was sacked, unceremoniously and without the courtesy of John Lawrence doing it.

Stein wasn't just lifting the title: he epitomized the new breed of track-suited, tactical trainers who almost mocked by their presence the starched, anachronistic three-piece-suited managers of what was becoming a bygone era. Symon, of course, belonged to that time, but his departure was hastened by a catastrophic 1–0 defeat – at Berwick Rangers in the first round of the Scottish Cup in 1967.

The defeat became a black day for Rangers fans all over the world, but at least it had some good in it, given that Berwick's goalkeeper and player-coach was Jock Wallace himself. Symon was sacked unceremoniously the following November when the team was unbeaten and leading the League – but since when did football have any rules?

Davy White had a short spell as manager – too short to tell if he would have been any good, and too long for the liking of Rangers' directors. European quarter and semi-finals, only losing the League on the last day of the season – disaster; not good enough; time to go. Willie Waddell, one-time flying winger at Ibrox, took over. Between that day and his death in 1992, Waddell became one of the club's most distinguished and pivotal thinkers.

As the team moved on, first of all to win European glory in 1972, and then finally to end Celtic's seemingly-incessant stream of title victories, Waddell judged that his role was further up the club hierarchy. It is never easy to hand over power, especially such heady power as running the team you love and used to play for, but Waddell judged that the modern trends of the game needed a younger coach and Jock Wallace was promoted immediately after the Cup-Winners' Cup win of 1972.

Jim BAXTER

Perhaps it is a prerequisite of any true Rangers great that he has a nickname, but Jim Baxter will always be known as "Slim". When he arrived at Rangers from Raith Rovers in June 1960 he was impossibly slim and unfeasibly talented. Blessed with a genius's ball skills and the arrogance to use them to entertain the crowd while still winning the game, Baxter is unique in the Scottish history of midfielders. The king of cool in the 1960s, when Mod was in, he along with Denis Law, Paddy Crerand, Billy McNeill and a cast of other Old Firm dudes were probably Europe's coolest players – pork-pie hats, shades and razor-sharp suits. So good was he that by 1963 he was picked in a World Select to play England; but a year later Rapid Vienna's Skocik slaughtered him in a tackle during a European victory inspired by Baxter and that fractured right shinbone was a blight on his career. But in 1967 it was Baxter who orchestrated that 3–2 win for Scotland at Wembley, when he taunted the World Champions by playing keepy-uppy and sitting on the ball. The first man to climb Ibrox's stairs and demand a wage rise, Baxter's time at Ibrox was split by a four-year spell at Sunderland and Forest. But he won three Leagues, four Cups and 34 Scotland caps in a wonderfully exuberant career.

Part of Waddell's decision was based around the tragic events of 2 January 1971. The crush on Stairway 13 killed 66 people in the most cruel fashion. For hours it was not clear who had lived and who had died: so horrendous were the injuries sustained that identification was difficult.

Families were split, friends lost, and all for no good reason. So Waddell dedicated himself to the invention of the greatest stadium Rangers had it in themselves to build, and today they have it. Wallace not only led the team he inherited to the treble in 1975–76 and 1977–78; he also won Rangers their first title for 11 years when the Premier Division was founded and Celtic had been chasing their 10th consecutive championship.

That alone would have made him an all-time legend. But he was an ex-King's Own Scottish Borderer and barked new levels of fitness into his team, which then dominated the Seventies. His shrewdest introductions to the squad included greats such as Davie Cooper, Tam Forsyth, Bobby Russell and Gordon Smith, and it was a shock when he left abruptly for Leicester, having completed the treble in the Scottish Cup Final of 1978 against Aberdeen.

Legend succeeded legend as John Greig took over as boss, but it was a bad time to be in charge of the club from which he had just retired as a player. Cups were won regularly under Greig and there was one delightful European run, in 1978–79, but the squad was partly ageing and partly unable to cope with the challenges of the New Firm and Billy McNeill's rejuvenated Celtic.

Ibrox stadium was being rebuilt – always a traumatic time – and somehow Bill Struth's tenet that Rangers should always regard themselves as first bar none slipped away without it seeming to matter very much. Crowds were down to 6-7,000, and even the return of Jock Wallace, in the 1983–84 season, could not halt the decline. Between 1978 and 1985, six trophies were won – not a bad record at all – but Rangers were hibernating.

They were abruptly woken in 1986, by David Holmes and Graeme Souness immediately making improbable grand signings, winning the title for the first time in nine seasons, attracting the brilliant brain of David Murray and starting the astonishing revival which, in 1997, brought them parity with Celtic's nine-in-a-row record.

Jim Baxter and trophies went together like hand and glove: Slim Jim, the way he will always be remembered by the Ibrox fans

Chapter 2
Nine-in-a-Row

All astonishing records must start somewhere: but who, in August 1988, thought Rangers were on the verge of their greatest glory?

One down, 1988–89

19 JULY: Gary Stevens is a superb-value £1 million signing from Everton this day: he goes on to make 187 League appearances for the club.

13 AUGUST: Stevens scores on his debut, against Hamilton, the first goal of "Nine-in-a-row". A total of 672 goals later, Brian Laudrup heads home the winner against Dundee United – the clincher of that ninth title. Rangers win 2–0 at Douglas Park this day with McCoist (who else?) getting the second.

27 AUGUST: The first sign that something extraordinary is about to happen: Rangers 5, Celtic 1, the biggest Rangers win for over 20 years despite Frank McAvennie opening the scoring. Souness's team-talk is, according to John Brown, "like nothing I had ever heard before or since", and McCoist (2), Wilkins, Drinkell and Walters send most of the 42,000-strong crowd home in ecstasies.

27 SEPTEMBER: A marvellous month of four straight League wins for the Ger as the side warms to the task Motherwell 0–2 (Drinkell, Durrant), Hearts 1–2 (Durrant (pen), Nisbet), St Mirren 2–1 (D Cooper (pen), Walters) and, on this day, Dundee United 0–1 (I Ferguson).

A phenomenon within a phenomenon: without McCoist, could Rangers have won Nine-in-a-row?

8 OCTOBER: A horrific afternoon for which there is no explanation, as Neil Simpson's tackle puts Ian Durrant out of the game for more than two years. Rangers lose 2–1 to a Charlie Nicholas header at Pittodrie.

23 OCTOBER: With controversy still raging over that tackle, the League Cup Final is free from retribution and is the second of three classic finals between the two sides in consecutive seasons. Davie Dodds, later to play and coach at Ibrox, scores twice for Aberdeen, but a McCoist double, including the winner, and one from Ian Ferguson win the Cup.

Still one of Scottish football's most controversial tackles: Durrant writhes as Simpson walks away

9 NOVEMBER: Kevin Drinkell's solitary goal is not enough to prevent an aggregate 3–1 defeat by Cologne, 1–1 on the night. Rangers go out of Europe.

12 NOVEMBER: Celtic's revenge takes less than three months: a 3–1 win at Parkhead. Once again, Mark Walters scores for Rangers.

23 NOVEMBER: One of the most significant days of the century for Rangers Football Club as David Murray engineers a brilliant coup – buying the club from Lawrence Marlborough for £6 million. A personal friend of Graeme Souness, Murray has taken four weeks to put the deal together after his old hometown club of Ayr United amazingly fails to accept his £500,000 bid to buy them out. Souness takes a 10 per cent stake in Rangers and Murray says: "I do not see myself as the owner of Rangers Football Club. I am the custodian of one of Scotland's greatest institutions … I have never been content with second place in the business world and I won't be in football."

26 NOVEMBER: Having pledged to stay away from Ibrox to let things settle down, while admitting that "Saturday cannot come quickly enough", Murray sees his team win their first match with him as owner – a Richard Gough drive beats Aberdeen 1–0.

3 JANUARY: The astonishing Old Firm tally at Ibrox reaches "Rangers: scored 9, conceded 2" with a 4–1 win which restarts the New Year celebrations all over again. Celtic lead through Chris Morris, but Butcher, Ian Ferguson and Walters (2) complete another thrashing.

David Murray: able to bring the good times back and make Rangers financially mighty

7 JANUARY: A surprise of a different kind as Motherwell win 2–1 at Fir Park, but it sparks a 12-match unbeaten run which will take Rangers to the title.

28 JANUARY: Raith Rovers 1, Rangers 1 – the first of Rangers' eight matches in the Scottish Cup. It will be their largest number of matches in the Scottish Cup without winning it since 1953–54, something which has only happened on one other occasion – in 1921–22.

1 FEBRUARY: The replay is won 3–0 thanks to Walters, Drinkell and Ian Ferguson.

11 FEBRUARY: Controversy erupts: Souness clashes with a linesman and is banned from the touchline until the end of the season, with a £100 fine thrown in for good measure.

25 FEBRUARY: Goals from Ian Ferguson, McCoist and Walters bring a 3–0 home win over St Mirren: it is the start of a mini-Nine-in-a-Row as Rangers win their next eight League matches, scoring 17 goals.

21 MARCH: Having beaten Stranraer 8–0 in the last round, Dundee United provide matches four and five in the Scottish Cup with this 2–2 draw at Ibrox (Drinkell, McCoist) and the 0–1 win at Tannadice six days later (McCoist).

1 APRIL: No fools in blue, as Rangers go to Parkhead and win 2–1 – their first win there for nine years. Drinkell and Ferguson score for Rangers (already their 12th against Celtic this season) and Walker for Celtic.

15 APRIL: The 0–0 Scottish Cup semi-final draw is overshadowed when Souness, after his phone link to the dugout is suddenly cut, ignores his ban by twice going to the touchline to pass instructions to Walter Smith. The SFA believes it to be a heinous act.

18 APRIL: Three days previously, St Johnstone had performed above themselves to draw 0–0 at Hampden in the Scottish Cup semi-final. This time Rangers play to form, winning 4–0 thanks to Walters (his 17th of the season), Stevens, Drinkell and McCoist. Rangers are now to face Celtic at Hampden in the Scottish Cup Final on 20 May for the treble.

27 APRIL: The SFA put the world to rights by banning Souness from the touchline until the end of 1989–90 and fining him £2,000.

22 APRIL: A title-winning 2–0 at St Mirren: the glory goes to Ian Ferguson and Ally McCoist. One in a row.

29 APRIL: Rangers celebrate their second Championship in three seasons by beating Hearts 4–0 courtesy of two English men – Mel Sterland and Kevin Drinkell – with two apiece.

6 MAY: Andy Gray completes the 12-game unbeaten run, comprising 11 wins, 26 goals scored and only six conceded, by getting both goals in a 2–1 defeat of Dundee at Dens Park. The powerful surge has given Rangers one-in-a-row and it is Gray's last full appearance for the club. Sky TV beckons, eventually.

20 MAY: Hard to believe that it is the consistent Gary Stevens who falters, muffing a Celtic throw-in and allowing Joe Miller freedom to score the winner: the Scottish Cup goes to the other half of the Old Firm and the treble is lost.

Back-to-back, 1989–90

12 JULY: Glasgow's "best" rumour proves to be true, shocking even those who had been peddling it, and Maurice Johnston has opted not to join his former club, Celtic, despite being paraded in a green-and-white jersey at a "signing" ceremony. He signs for Rangers instead. There is some confusion in Glasgow.

29 JULY: Mo Johnston plays in a Rangers jersey for the first time in a testimonial at Airdrie.

12 AUGUST: After the title flag is unfurled, St Mirren confound all reasonable expectation by winning 0–1. But, in scoring, Kenny McDowell's challenge is reminiscent of bygone days; Chris Woods sustains a dislocated shoulder.

19 AUGUST: In the intervening period, with Israeli international Bonni Ginzburg in goal, Rangers have beaten Arbroath 4–0 in the League Cup. But Hibs win 2–0 at Easter Road on this day. Rangers haven't started with two defeats for 12 years, when coincidentally the second defeat was also 2–0 to Hibs: Rangers then went on to win the title!

One down **1988–89** – *Back-to-back* **1989–90** • 17

If there was one match in which Mo Johnston had to win his doubters over it was vs. Celtic: and he did

26 AUGUST: Spirits are raised with a 1–1 draw at Parkhead. Not only do Celtic require a late, untidy equalizer, but Mo Johnston is given so much stick by the home crowd that most Rangers fans are forced to accept him as "one of them". A turning-point all round.

9 SEPTEMBER: Repayment: Mo's headed winner, for Rangers' first victory of the Championship defence, against Aberdeen.

13 SEPTEMBER: Europe is already over after a 1–3 first-leg defeat by Bayern Munich – Walters is the solitary scorer – followed by a 0-0 draw in the second leg in Bavaria.

22 OCTOBER: After almost as good a draw as could be hoped for – Arbroath, Morton, Hamilton, Dunfermline – Rangers' 14-goal romp to the League Cup Final ends in yet another superb tussle with Aberdeen. Despite a Walters penalty, two Paul Mason goals win it for the Dons.

28 OCTOBER: All managers plead for time: few are given it. An example of how important that is comes when McCoist and Johnston blend as a partnership at the beginning of this month, after only eight weeks playing together. Wins against Dundee United, St Mirren and Hibs come from four McCoist goals and three from MoJo.

4 NOVEMBER: Johnston gains as much acceptance as he ever will with a real striker's goal against Celtic in the final minute at Ibrox. It is vital for both him and Rangers.

25 NOVEMBER: Emotion rules as Ray Wilkins is given a fantastic ovation for his last game, a 3–0 win over Dunfermline.

9 DECEMBER: With the second in a 3–1 win over Motherwell, Ally McCoist scores Rangers' 7,000th Scottish League goal.

30 DECEMBER: Rangers draw 0-0 at Easter Road with Hibs: an unremarkable game except for another good display between the Hibernian posts by one Andrew Lewis Goram. Notes are taken.

2 JANUARY: The team is motoring now, on a six-game unbeaten run, and add Celtic's scalp with an extremely rare goal from Nigel Spackman.

25 FEBRUARY: But revenge is swift and Celtic win 1–0 in the Scottish Cup fourth round at Parkhead.

24 MARCH: Rangers have not been beaten in the League for four months, but Goram again keeps a clean sheet, Hibs win 1–0 and there is pressure leading up to the last Celtic match of the season.

1 APRIL: Walters scores a penalty; Johnston lashes in a volley; McCoist, with another penalty, beats Derek Johnstone's post-war scoring record for the club of 131 goals; and Rangers beat Celtic 3–0. Rangers are now unbeaten in six consecutive Old Firm matches.

21 APRIL: 20 days later and it is the title which is won, 0–1 at Tannadice, when Trevor Steven's header beats Dundee United. Two-in-a-row.

Hat-trick, 1990–91

19 JULY: Mark Hateley signs from AS Monaco for £1 million. The fifth-to-last signing Souness makes – and unquestionably one of his best-ever. 169 League appearances in total, and 88 goals.

8 AUGUST: Pieter Huistra follows Hateley for a quarter of the sum. But the former Twente winger is responsible for supplying many of the Englishman's headers. A popular acquisition: 126 League appearances in total, 22 goals.

15 SEPTEMBER: Terry Hurlock's shot equalizes a header from Derek Whyte and the Old Firm derby is a draw.

22 SEPTEMBER: Terry Butcher's career with Rangers comes to an end, although no one yet realizes this is the case, when he heads an own-goal against Dundee United in a 2–1 defeat at Tannadice. A great captain is about to move on.

13 OCTOBER: Oleg Kuznetsov, the brilliant Russian international sweeper, makes his Rangers debut in a 5–0 win over St Mirren at Ibrox, after signing from Dynamo Kiev. He plays majestically but needs to enjoy it while he can.

Shocking though his exit was, Souness was just another great name who was not bigger than the club

20 OCTOBER: Kuznetsov is carried off after a challenge from a St Johnstone player. Knee ligament damage is confirmed and he doesn't play for the first team again for nearly a year. The game ends 0–0.

26 OCTOBER: Graeme Souness and Butcher disagree about whether the player is or is not fit to play in Sunday's League Cup Final. Butcher insists he is "injured", Souness claims the player has "refused to play".

24 OCTOBER: Out of the European Cup, basically, after a 3–0 mauling in Belgrade by a very good Red Star team.

28 OCTOBER: Rangers win the final 2–1 against Celtic in the most dramatic fashion. Paul Elliot gives Celtic the lead, Walters equalizes, and then Richard Gough, in his first final as captain, turns penalty-box poacher for the winner. Souness defies his ban and celebrates on the pitch with the players.

6 NOVEMBER: In a press conference at Ibrox, Souness announces Butcher's availability for transfer.

25 NOVEMBER: McCoist, unaffected by the depressing regularity of a place on the bench, comes on to score the winner at Parkhead after Johnston and Paul Elliot had made it 1–1. Rangers are now unbeaten in eight Old Firm League matches.

2 JANUARY: Championship-winning form around the turn of the year, as always: Rangers have won four and drawn one since the last meeting with Celtic. Walters and Hateley both score to secure a 2–0 win at Ibrox. Now unbeaten in nine Old Firm matches.

2 MARCH: A 15-game unbeaten run since mid-November ends at Pittodrie; but, significantly, there have been seven consecutive wins in that run – insurance against Aberdeen's own impressive form.

17 MARCH: Mad March continues with havoc at Parkhead. Three Englishmen, Walters, Hateley and Hurlock, are all sent off against Celtic, who lose Peter Grant but win 2–0 in the Scottish Cup quarter-final. Another Englishman, Trevor Steven, is injured and will not play again this season.

24 MARCH: Missing the four casualties of the Battle of Parkhead, Rangers lose an Old Firm League match for the first time since 12 November 1988. The 0–3 scoreline is a real body-blow.

16 APRIL: An absolute sensation topping anything since Souness's arrival from Sampdoria in 1986, as it is

Mayhem follows Hateley's brilliant header in the title-winning match vs. Aberdeen in May 1991

announced that Souness has been told by David Murray to clear his desk and leave because of his wish to accept the Liverpool job, vacant since Kenny Dalglish walked out of Anfield. A provisional agreement that Souness can see out the Scottish season is immediately abandoned when the news is leaked in England, and Murray calls his friend's decision "the biggest mistake of his life". Bookies make Dalglish a 4–6 favourite, but players at Ibrox are made aware very quickly that Walter Smith, who enjoys the confidence of both his squad and his chairman, will be the next in charge.

19 APRIL: At a press conference it is announced that Walter Smith (who according to Richard Gough has "over the last four or five years been doing most of the work anyway") is to be the new Rangers manager. Meanwhile the club prepares to pay Manchester United £75,000 for Archie Knox to become Number Two to Smith at Ibrox.

20 APRIL: Walter Smith is officially in charge for the first time as Rangers keep their two-point margin over Aberdeen by winning 0–1 at Love Street against St Mirren. The goal comes from a cute overhead kick by youngster Sandy Robertson.

4 MAY: The wheels come off in a comprehensive 3–0 defeat at Motherwell, who win courtesy of goals from Philliben and Arnott (2) while Mark Walters chooses a bad time to miss a penalty. Rangers and Aberdeen are now equal at the top of the League and due to play one another at Ibrox seven days later. Two ruinous breakaway strikes from Arnott mean goal difference favours the Dons: a draw next week will win them the League.

11 MAY: Scottish football has rarely been in such a fever. Aberdeen name a slightly-defensive side but have chances, notably from Van de Ven, to open the scoring and put a massive grip on the championship trophy. Instead, Walters conjures some magic on the left, launches the ball towards the box and Hateley scores one of Ibrox's most significant goals ever, with a beautiful header. He adds the second, and Rangers have the title. Three-in-a-row.

27 JUNE: Andy Goram makes his £1 million move from Hibs. Rangers have a world-class Scottish goalkeeper who makes 160 League appearances for them, while becoming one of the finest keepers ever in Scotland's history.

Four-in-a-row, 1991–92

2 JULY: David Robertson joins Rangers from Aberdeen for a fee of £900,000. Total League appearances 184, goals 15.

5 AUGUST: Alexei Mikhailichenko moves from Serie A to the Premier League for £2 million, three years and 10 months after first playing at Ibrox – for Dynamo Kiev in the European Cup. Total appearances 110, goals 20.

13 AUGUST: Trevor Steven scores in a 3–1 win over Motherwell, his last game before a £5.5 million move to Marseille. He proves a shrewd investment: Rangers' profit on the sale is £4 million.

15 AUGUST: Stuart McCall signs from Everton for £1.2 million. 163 total League appearances, 15 goals.

31 AUGUST: Hateley, now that the fans love him, rewards them with both goals in a muscular 0–2 win at Parkhead.

8 SEPTEMBER: Alexei "Chenks" Mikhailitchenko makes his Premier League debut against Falkirk in a 2–0 victory.

25 SEPTEMBER: Keith Wright capitalizes on a rare Goram mistake to head the winner for Hibernian in the League Cup semi-final at Hampden. Rangers, the holders, are out.

2 OCTOBER: Out of Europe, courtesy of Sparta Prague, but only thanks to a defensive mistake in extra time with Rangers about to go through 2–1 on aggregate after a McCall double. The away goal wins it again.

29 OCTOBER: It must have been hard for McCoist not to celebrate the departure of Graeme Souness. In a wasted season, 1990–91, he only started 10 League games, scoring four times. This day saw him score his ninth goal in October, albeit in a 3–2 defeat by Dundee United. But all his other goals had been in wins. It is Mo Johnston's last game for Rangers before moving to Everton.

2 NOVEMBER: The point is underscored when McCoist scores to take a 1–1 draw from Celtic at Ibrox.

4 DECEMBER: Although the run starts the previous Saturday with a 2–0 win over Motherwell, it is the barnstorming 2–3 win at Pittodrie which gets the Rangers engine going. Hateley opens the scoring and then does untold damage to the confidence and reputation of Aberdeen's defence, simply turning David Winnie near the half-way line and tearing away from him like Linford Christie before thumping the second. Aberdeen fight back but McCoist wins it with a curving chip.

21 DECEMBER: After 17 months and £20 million of investment, Ibrox's Club Deck opens for business, full of debenture holders who have guaranteed their seats: they watch Ally McCoist score his 20th and 21st goals of the season in a 2–0 win over Dundee United. Super Ally scoring is a sight they will see another 18 times in competitive matches this season.

24 DECEMBER: Rangers make a decent investment by agreeing a new four-year contract with Ally McCoist. Between now and May 1997, McCoist is to score 119 goals for the club he loves – a total most players would dream of scoring in an entire career. Six of them come against Celtic, 10 in semi-finals or finals of the cups and two against Leeds, to make Rangers the first British club to play in the Champions' League. Merry Christmas, Ally.

1 JANUARY: Ne'erday derbies on 1 January? An increasing rarity; but not so Rangers' 3–1 win, which comes from McCoist, Hateley's penalty and a long-range thump from John Brown.

21 MARCH: The 16-game unbeaten run, which started back in November against Motherwell, is comprehensively ended by Celtic in a 2–0 win. But 14 of those games have been wins. Championship form around the turn of the year – again.

31 MARCH: Revenge 10 days later. Not the most thrilling but certainly the most titanic of struggles, as Rangers draw on resources they never knew they had to beat Celtic 1–0 in the Scottish Cup semi-final, despite being reduced to 10 men after only six minutes when David Robertson is sent off for a body-check on former team-mate Joe Miller. Robertson has been

St Mirren go down 4–0 at Ibrox: party time for 40,000 as Rangers make it four, and still want more

ribbed at Ibrox ever since Miller starred in the game a week and half ago. But a superb tackle by McCall in midfield and then a finish on the run by McCoist give Rangers what is undoubtedly one of their most satisfying wins in recent years. Now Airdrie await them in the final.

18 APRIL: Dropping only one point between the Celtic defeat in March and the end of the season, Rangers clinch the title on this day by thrashing St Mirren 4–0 at Ibrox, entrancing and delighting a crowd of 40,000. McCoist's 30th and 31st goals are added to by Steven and Huistra. Four-in-a-row.

9 MAY: For the first time in 11 years the Scottish Cup belongs to Rangers, after McCoist and Hateley score in a 2–1 win at Hampden.

4 JUNE: Dave McPherson, sold to Hearts by Rangers, signs for Rangers again for £1.3 million. Rangers will later re-sell him – to Hearts, of course. Total Nine-in-a-Row League appearances 70, goals 3.

Now it's five, 1992–93

2 JULY: Charlie Miller moves up from Rangers' Boys Club. This talented performer will captain the reserve side to many trophies.

29 JULY: One of Rangers' most unusual, and profitable, transfer sagas is completed as Trevor Steven rejoins the club just under a year after leaving to sign for Marseille. Having joined Rangers in 1989 for £1.5 million from Everton, he moved to Marseille in 1991 for £5.5 million, won the French championship and then signed for Rangers again in a £2.4 million transfer – after which he went on to play in two Champions' League draws against the French team he had just left.

15 AUGUST: In an astonishing match, Rangers lose 4–3 to Dundee at Dens Park. The result, and later comments from the Dundee manager Simon Stainrod are later identified by Ally McCoist as the spur to what becomes a massive 44-game unbeaten run which brings Rangers their first treble for 15 years and takes them to within a goal of the European Cup Final.

22 AUGUST: Rangers welcome Ian Durrant back to top form: his goal brings a 1–1 draw with Celtic.

30 SEPTEMBER: Lyngby is beaten in Denmark by a superb Durrant goal for a 3–0 aggregate win in the first Champions' League qualifier – Leeds are next.

21 OCTOBER: McAllister opens the scoring for the English champions with one of the best goals of his career, but McCoist and then a Lukic own-goal give Rangers a well-deserved win.

25 OCTOBER: Aberdeen are beaten 2–1 after extra-time in the League Cup Final at Hampden. McCall turns a Snelders fumble into the opener and, after Shearer equalizes, a Gary Smith own-goal wins it.

4 NOVEMBER: One of Rangers' best-ever results as Leeds are snuffed out of the second leg: Hateley and McCoist score excellent goals and Cantona's goal makes no difference whatsoever. The first British club through to the Champions League – 4–2 on aggregate.

11 NOVEMBER: 10 straight wins, 20 points, 35 goals and a 1–0 victory over Celtic, courtesy of Durrant, culminate in a 3–1 defeat of Dundee on this day.

25 NOVEMBER: Ripped apart by Marseilles, Rangers feel as if they have won when late equalizers from McSwegan and Hateley make the Ibrox crowd erupt. The 23rd unbeaten game this season in all competitions.

9 DECEMBER: Ian Ferguson's deflected shot brings a valuable away victory against CSKA Moscow, played in Bochum, Germany, due to bad weather in Moscow.

2 JANUARY: Nestling in the middle of a run of eight consecutive victories, Trevor Steven scores a header for a 1–0 Old Firm derby win.

3 MARCH: Brugge make it tough in Belgium and Gough, Stevens, Steven, Ferguson and Dale Gordon all miss the trip. Brugge preserve their five-year unbeaten run at home in Europe, but Huistra's goal means a valuable draw for Rangers. The 40th unbeaten match in all competitions this season for Walter Smith's team.

17 MARCH: The return leg is bad-tempered and Hateley is conned into getting himself sent off. Durrant scores another cracker, Stalens equalizes, then Scott Nisbet scores a goal so lucky it defies belief. But it is the winner.

20 MARCH: At last the unbeaten run ends, in the 46th game, when Celtic win 2–1 at Parkhead. It is already Nisbet's last game for Rangers.

7 APRIL: In Marseilles, Rangers find the French formidably good; but after losing the first goal, Durrant again scores a superb half-volley from the edge of the box. 1–1, and the final is still in view.

21 APRIL: Not until the last of what seem like a thousand chances slips away from Rangers does the European Cup Final do so too. A 0–0 draw against Moscow is not enough and Rangers' best European campaign for 20 years ends in tears.

28 APRIL: Scotland play one of the most infamous games in the history of Rangers Football Club. During the 5–0 defeat in Portugal, Ally McCoist breaks his leg particularly badly in a challenge with Oceano – a vicious turn of luck for the striker, who has reached 49 goals for the season to see the only chance of a half-century he will ever have disappearing in the blink of an eye. This is also Richard Gough's last appearance

No one deserves to clutch this trophy more than Smith, whose 1992–93 season is his best to date

Rangers win the treble at Parkhead: Aberdeen are second in the Cup, as in both other competitions

for Scotland, as his simmering relationship with Andy Roxburgh reaches boiling point. Gough has won 62 caps and leads Rangers to five subsequent championships.

1 MAY: McSwegan's goal in a 1–0 win over Airdrie also wins the title. Five-in-a-row.

8 MAY: The champions win their last home game of the season, in front of more than 42,000 delerious fans, beating Dundee United for the third time with a goal from Huistra. The injured McCoist is carried on to the pitch for after-match celebrations by Ian Ferguson. Strapped to McCoist's back is a cardboard cut-out of himself – but with Ollie Reed's head added. Perhaps it is a reference to McCoist's acting ability. Perhaps not.

9 MAY: As Ibrox is resurfaced in a massive operation, chunks of the championship-winning turf are sold to fans as part of a charity fund-raising scheme. Ally McCoist's goals are re-enacted in back gardens all over Scotland.

13 MAY: Trevor Steven's damaged Achilles tendon requires an operation, and the influential midfielder will miss the Scottish Cup Final against Aberdeen at Parkhead. His last game of the season has been against CSKA Moscow.

26 MAY: Soon-to-be-disgraced Marseille genuinely shock the footballing world by winning the European Cup, beating Milan 1–0 courtesy of a headed goal from Basile Boli.

29 MAY: The treble is clinched at Rangers' new happy hunting ground – Parkhead. Hampden Park's renovation means that Celtic's stadium will become the place where Rangers regularly win trophies. Aberdeen are the beaten Scottish Cup finalists, just as they finished second in the League and were beaten finalists after extra time in the League Cup Final too. Neil Murray opens the scoring with a deflection off Irvine, and Hateley scores his 29th goal of the season before half-time. Richardson gets one for Aberdeen to make it 2–1. It has been a long haul; and after the previous season's League and Scottish Cup double, this treble makes it five consecutive trophies – a historic achievement.

Six! 1993–94

20 JULY: After a long tug-of-love between Dundee United, Leeds and Rangers, Duncan Ferguson eventually signs at Ibrox for £4 million. One or two foreign signings have failed to live up to their potential, but Ferguson proves the biggest disappointment. Aged 22, he has abundant talent, is Scottish (the three-for-eigner rule still being a factor), is dying to do well for Rangers and promises to be the mid or long-term replacement for Mark Hateley. Instead his time is beset with injuries, immaturity, controversy, an SFA ban and a jail sentence. Without question, however, his arrival inspires the Englishman to even greater heights: Rangers get 53 appearances, 30 goals and every last ounce of skill and enthusiasm from Hateley in a marvellous season. From Ferguson, the club gets 14 League appearances (six as sub) and two goals before he leaves for Everton and the Premiership.

27 JULY: Sad news for Nisbet. Medical experts end his career – the decision comes only four months after the greatest moment of his career, that brilliant goal against Brugge in the Champions' League.

3 AUGUST: Ally McCoist's testimonial against Newcastle is a huge success despite the man himself sitting it out, still grounded by the broken leg sustained against Portugal, and a 2–1 win for Newcastle. 42,623 fans attend to pay tribute to a man who cannot stop scoring for Rangers.

21 AUGUST: Duncan Ferguson makes his debut in a 0–0 draw with Celtic at Parkhead.

18 SEPTEMBER: The omens are already in place for what will be a hugely difficult season thanks to a variety of injury problems, as a five-game spell without a win culminates in a 0–2 defeat at Pittodrie. Rangers are in seventh position in the League, but it is the League debut for 17-year-old Charlie Miller. Already he is the 22nd player Walter Smith has had to use in the championship.

22 SEPTEMBER: Which makes it all the more outstanding when, only four days later, Rangers are reduced to 10 men in the Coca-Cola Cup semi-final after Pieter Huistra lashes out at Tom Boyd, but Ian Durrant and Mark Hateley combine to take advantage of Mike Galloway's mistake for a 1–0 victory over Celtic.

25 SEPTEMBER: It is the necessary boost. After three draws and two defeats in the League, Rangers beat Hibs 2–1 thanks to Steven and Hateley.

29 SEPTEMBER: However, their European ambitions crash calamitously in Sofia when, with Rangers only seconds from going through 4–3 on aggregate, Nikolei Todorov hits an improbably vicious long-range shot

So much more was expected from Duncan Ferguson: but his Old Firm debut was satisfactory

past Ally Maxwell. Rangers are out on away goals in the first round.

24 OCTOBER: A moment to sum up McCoist. Durrant scores first in the League Cup Final at Parkhead but Rangers are still off-form and McPherson's own-goal adds to the nerves. McCoist, on the bench, has barely recovered from his broken leg and is not fit, but Smith somehow gets it spot-on by putting on his substitute, who scores with a typically dazzling overhead kick to win the Cup.

30 OCTOBER: Mistakes by Maxwell – Goram is still a long way from recovering from his operation – help Celtic to a 1–2 win at Ibrox. McCoist scores.

23 NOVEMBER: Gordon Durie signs for Rangers from Tottenham Hotspur. He repays the £1.2 million investment handsomely with a total of 87 League appearances and 39 goals.

11 DECEMBER: The lowest point for Rangers in many months. Dundee United defeat them comprehensively at Ibrox 3–0 and Ferguson is sent off for spitting at Petric.

22 DECEMBER: David Murray's Christmas present to the fans is the announcement that Ibrox's development continues at an incredible pace: the corners of the stadium are to be completed with seating and giant television screens utilizing the most up-to-date technology.

1 JANUARY: Probably the most important 90 minutes of the championship. Celtic are strong favourites to win at home, but thanks to Hateley and Miko, who gets two, Rangers are 3–0 up within half an hour. Kuznetsov scores with a thrilling volley and the game finishes 4–2.

16 APRIL: The game which will bring the end of Duncan Ferguson's Rangers career, earn him a ban and put him in Barlinnie high-security prison. He is accused of headbutting Jock McStay. Ferguson also scores in a 4–0 win.

26 APRIL: With 20 unbeaten games since the New Year's Day derby, Rangers finally drop two points – to their nearest challengers, Motherwell. McCoist scores in a 2–1 defeat.

3 MAY: Despite the huge disappointment of losing 0–1 at Easter Road to Keith Wright's goal, Rangers clinch their sixth successive title – a marvellous achievement given the injury toll which followed the heroics of the 1992–93 season. Six-in-a-row.

9 MAY: Duncan Ferguson's disciplinary hearing is held in front of the SFA committee at Park Gardens. Jock McStay fails to show up.

12 MAY: Ferguson is given a massive 12-match ban by the SFA. They are sternly criticized in many quarters for having risked prejudicing the Procurator Fiscal's investigation into the incident and Ferguson's subsequent court appearance.

21 MAY: A second consecutive treble, and Rangers' eighth trophy out of nine is up for grabs against Dundee United in the Scottish Cup Final. It is a close-run match, but most players are physically and mentally drained and United's late goal wins it.

Seventh heaven, 1994–95

5 JULY: Basile Boli signs from Marseille for £2.7 million.

21 JULY: Walter Smith's best signing, Brian Laudrup, puts pen to paper, signs from Fiorentina for a bargain £2.5 million and sets about entrancing the Rangers fans, the media and opposition defenders.

27 JULY: First game for Lauders: a 1–1 draw against Aalborg in his home country of Denmark.

29 JULY: The Rangers stage show, *Follow Follow,* opens at the King's Theatre in Glasgow, portraying the club's 122-year history in words and song.

10 AUGUST: Rangers lose 0–2 in an incredibly hostile match against AEK Athens. Two goals from Dimitris Saravakos win the match. Incredibly, Athens are not punished for rockets and flares fired by their fans into the travelling Scottish support. To qualify for the Champions' League, Rangers will have to produce their most exceptional European performance for years.

Motherwell get the first sight of a dance defenders will be doing frequently: they call it "The Laudrup"

13 AUGUST: Laudrup makes his home League debut, dribbling most of the length of the pitch to set up Duncan Ferguson for a rare goal – the winner, in fact. Another Rangers legend is born and Laudrup becomes the darling of Ibrox.

24 AUGUST: David Murray bills the return leg "one of the toughest challenges this team has ever faced". He is correct; after a night of frustration, AEK get the vital opener through Toni Savevski and are never likely to concede defeat after that.

27 AUGUST: Another Old Firm clash at Ibrox, and a black day for Rangers. The goals come from Paul McStay and a brilliant John Collins free kick. It is Rangers' second home defeat by Celtic in less than a year.

31 AUGUST: Scottish football is shocked as Rangers lose 2–1 at home to Falkirk in the League Cup. The holders are out, this time thanks to quality finishing from Richard Cadette, despite Brian Laudrup's first goal for the club.

11 SEPTEMBER: Few wins at Ibrox in recent years are as welcome as the 3–0 demolition of Hearts. A Hateley double and one for Durie stop the rot and Rangers are back at the races.

15 SEPTEMBER: A stormy chapter ends with Duncan Ferguson's loan to Everton. He will later move there in a profitable £4.26 million transfer. Ian Durrant accompanies him to Goodison on loan, but returns to see out his contract with Rangers.

22 OCTOBER: Motherwell emerge as the only credible challengers with a 2–1 win at Fir Park on this day.

30 OCTOBER: But another challenge brings another superb result against Celtic. At Hampden Park, where Celtic are waiting for Parkhead to be reconstructed, Hateley scores twice and Laudrup shows magic for the

No club is immune, but McCoist particularly enjoys scoring against Aberdeen

third. 3–1, and an Old Firm debut win for Alan McLaren.

23 NOVEMBER: Ally McCoist picks up another medal, this time his MBE from Prince Charles at Buckingham Palace.

25 NOVEMBER: Then he scores his 299th goal in a 1–0 victory over perennial challengers Aberdeen at Ibrox.

29 DECEMBER: Pieter Huistra's transfer to San Frecce Hiroshima of Japan's J League is concluded. He costs the Japanese £500,000.

31 DECEMBER: Hogmanay happiness as Rangers beat Motherwell 3–1 to complete a month of four straight wins, three of which are away from home, with 10 goals scored. Dundee United (away), Kilmarnock (away) and Hibs (home) are the other victims. Rangers are on championship form in the festive period – again.

14 JANUARY: Huistra's last game: two goals, a 3–2 win over Falkirk and a huge ovation.

21 JANUARY: The first month of the New Year also passes unbeaten with draws against Celtic (1–1 at Ibrox) and Partick Thistle, then wins over Falkirk and, on this day, Hearts (1–0).

27 JANUARY: Rangers make a double purchase of Gary Bollan and Alec Cleland from Dundee United for £750,000.

12 FEBRUARY: Four months after their last defeat, the run ends with a surprising 2–0 loss to relegation-threatened Aberdeen.

20 FEBRUARY: Not a good month, Hearts play well to win 4–2 in the Scottish Cup fourth round. Laudrup and Durie score.

23 MARCH: The saddest day in Rangers' nine-championship run, as Ibrox legend Davie Cooper is pronounced dead after being struck down by a massive brain haemorrhage the previous day while teaching young kids the joys of playing football skilfully. A genuinely brilliant player, Cooper had been an integral part of all-conquering Rangers sides and also had to bear the burden of being in certain Ibrox teams when he was the only legitimate inheritor of the club's proud legacy. A left-winger of sublime balance, ball control and vision, goals such as his mind-boggling free kick against Aberdeen in the League Cup Final of 1987 and his Maradona-esque ball-juggling before scoring against Celtic in the Dryburgh Cup Final of 1979 are fitting memorials. His record with the club: Played 643; Championships 3; Scottish Cups 3; League Cups 7; Scotland Caps 22.

16 APRIL: Victory over Hibs at Ibrox, 3–1, wins the title as Motherwell's challenge evaporates. Durie, Durrant and Mikhailitchenko let the good times roll. Seven-in-a-row.

Eight! 1995–96

10 JULY: Rumours circulating since April are confirmed as Rangers beat Chelsea, Aston Villa and Sheffield Wednesday to the signing of Paul Gascoigne from Lazio for £4.3 million. Total League appearances in his first two seasons 54, goals 27.

20 JULY: Oleg Salenko follows from Valencia for £2.5 million. Total League appearances 16, goals 7.

29 JULY: Gordan Petric is next from Dundee United for £1.5 million under the noses of Celtic. Total League appearances 60, goals 3.

29 JULY: Having scored in previous friendlies around Scotland and Denmark, Gazza gets a goal on his Ibrox debut – in a 4–0 challenge-match victory over Steau Bucharest.

9 AUGUST: An extremely difficult night brings a one-goal lead over Anorthosis Famagusta to take to Cyprus. Durie is the predator who brings the Champions' League within sight after two barren seasons.

19 AUGUST: Gascoigne scores on his competitive home debut in a 3–0 League Cup win over Morton.

23 AUGUST: Gascoigne, admitting to team mates that he is almost too nervous to play, is substituted as Rangers efficiently draw 0–0 and qualify for the Champions' League.

19 SEPTEMBER: Parkhead hosts one of the most thrilling Old Firm matches in recent times as Rangers win the Coca-Cola Cup quarter-final 0–1. McStay peppers the Rangers goal but Andy Goram puts on one of his best-ever displays, as does Richard Gough. Paul Gascoigne's Old Firm debut ends with him clipping a superb back-post cross on to the head of Ally McCoist for the winner.

13 SEPTEMBER: Bucharest beat Rangers 1–0 at home in the first match of the Champions' League. McLaren is sent off.

23 SEPTEMBER: After three straight League wins, Rangers go down to a Darren Jackson penalty at Ibrox against Hibs. Rangers will not lose again in the championship for 20 matches.

27 SEPTEMBER: Dortmund visit and look dominant until half-time when Gascoigne re-emerges as a new man. His outstanding performance brings a 2–2 draw and nearly gains Rangers the victory. The goals are supplied by Ferguson and Gough.

30 SEPTEMBER: A clinical Rangers victory at Parkhead: Cleland's header just before half-time, and Gascoigne's lone run from the halfway line with a neat finish, bring a 2–0 victory.

12 OCTOBER: Duncan Ferguson is sent to Barlinnie Jail for the head-butt on Jock McStay.

One of Richard Gough's best-ever displays included this September 1995 goal against Borussia Dortmund

18 OCTOBER: Out of touch with the very best: Juventus 4, Rangers 1. Gough scores against the eventual European Cup winners.

24 OCTOBER: Aberdeen play with more flair – and luck – than Rangers to inflict a 2–1 defeat in the League Cup semi-final. Salenko is the scorer.

1 NOVEMBER: A better display, but no goals and very tired individual performances, making the scoreline a bit out of kilter with the match, by the end of a bruising fortnight. Rangers 0, Juventus 4.

11 NOVEMBER: Rangers 1, Aberdeen 1. So lousy is the match that a report goes to the Procurator Fiscal of Glasgow. Gascoigne is one of those mentioned. Salenko scores for Rangers.

12 NOVEMBER: Walter Smith is in Brazil to watch Jardel play for Gremio.

19 NOVEMBER: Millions watch on live television as the Old Firm play out a hugely entertaining 3–3 draw. It serves notice that Celtic are the main challengers for the first time since 1988. Laudrup, McCoist and McKinlay (og) score for Rangers and Goram produces a brilliant instinctive save from Van Hooijdonk.

22 NOVEMBER: Against Steau Bucharest, Gascoigne brings the house down with a run reminiscent of Gazza circa 1990 and a goal – but Ilie equalizes.

6 DECEMBER: Rangers again teeter on the brink of a terrific result but draw 2–2 in Dortmund on a rock-hard pitch. Gascoigne argues with Spanish referee Diaz Vega and is red-carded. Laudrup and Durie score.

30 DECEMBER: This is what the fans pay for: Rangers 7, Hibs 0. Four for Durie, one each for Salenko, Miller and Gazza, with a goal of lightning-quick feet and brain. Referee Dougie Smith should be ashamed, as he books Gazza for "booking" him after Smith drops his card.

20 JANUARY: Gough's injury needs treatment, Gazza is missing and Hearts win comprehensively at Ibrox 0–3. It obviously gets something out of the system, as the team then win six out of seven on the trot.

17 MARCH: The second successive Old Firm draw, after 0–0 at New Year, when McLaren's header is clawed back in the last minutes by one from Hughes.

7 APRIL: A Scottish Cup semi-final, and Laudrup makes the difference between Rangers and Celtic. He and McCoist score in a 2–1 win.

Chill out, Ref! Smith books Gazza for being happy

Against Aberdeen in April 1996, Gascoigne shows he still possesses genius with a stunning hat-trick

28 APRIL: Celtic have kept it arithmetically closer than any team since Aberdeen in 1991. It is the Dons against whom Rangers can win it and Gascoigne excels with a glorious hat-trick – right foot, left foot, penalty. Eight-in-a-row.

11 MAY: Richard Gough is awarded a testimonial in recognition of 10 seasons of brilliant service to the club. Arsenal are to be the opposition at the beginning of 1996–97.

15 MAY: Ally McCoist agrees another two-year deal at Ibrox after looking devastated at the thought of leaving whilst those around him celebrated the championship win, having beaten Aberdeen 3–1 almost three weeks previously. Offers from America, Switzerland and Japan are ignored.

18 MAY: Rangers excel themselves with one of the most devastating displays ever given in the Scottish Cup Final. Hearts are never in the game and lose 5–1; but despite Durie scoring the first Cup Final hat-trick since Dixie Deans managed the feat against Hibs in 1972, it will always be Laudrup's final. For a man who had already captivated Scotland with his skills, it says something that his 90 minutes in the final are widely regarded as some of the best football played in Scotland in the last two decades. As well as setting up Durie, Laudrup scores two of his own.

Durie's 1996 Scottish Cup Final hat-trick against Hearts came courtesy of the brilliant Laudrup

Nine-in-a-row, 1996–97

15 JULY: Joachim Bjorklund signs from Vicenza for £2.7 million. Total League appearances 29, goals 0.

16 JULY: Jorg Albertz signs from Hamburg for £4 million. Total League appearances 34, goals 10.

7 AUGUST: Alania Vladikavkaz give tricky moments but McInnes, McCoist and Petric win it 3–1. Champions' League football beckons.

21 AUGUST: An incredible night as Rangers score at will to beat Vladikavkaz in Russia 7–2. McCoist gets a hat-trick, Laudrup two and Van Vossen and Miller one each.

24 AUGUST: A delightful Gascoigne goal is the late winner at Ibrox against Dundee United.

11 SEPTEMBER: Unbeaten in all competitions, Rangers go to Switzerland and are thrashed 3–0 in the Champions' League by Grasshopper.

21 SEPTEMBER: The team's answer is an 11-goal, three-win sequence during which Hearts are reduced to seven men at Ibrox. This day Gazza scores twice in a 4–1 defeat of Kilmarnock.

25 SEPTEMBER: But Auxerre win 1–2 on the break at Ibrox. Another Gazza goal.

28 SEPTEMBER: Extra significance, then, in this Nine-in-a-Row season, for Celtic at Ibrox. Gough's header and a brilliant breakaway run and finish from Gascoigne win it.

19 OCTOBER: A 2–2 draw at home to Aberdeen steadies nerves after a stress-inducing build-up which includes a 4–1 defeat by Ajax, Gascoigne's sending-off, League defeat at Hibs and then the furore surrounding Gascoigne's private life. Gascoigne and Laudrup score.

22 OCTOBER: Rangers 6, Dunfermline 1 – at Celtic Park. Rangers love winning in the Cup – they particularly enjoy winning at Parkhead – and four goals shared between Laudrup and Andersen are the highlights of this semi-final.

25 January 1997: Sebastian Rozental's first goal

14 NOVEMBER: Once again Rangers are at Parkhead, and Celtic enter the match on top of the League. O'Neil slips, Laudrup attacks Stubbs who backs off and the Dane crashes one past Kerr. Two missed penalties and that miss from Van Vossen. A real landmark win.

24 NOVEMBER: Preceded by Rangers' first Champions' League win since 17 March 1993, 2–1 at home to Grasshoppers, the League Cup Final is a classic. Gascoigne's two goals in a 4–3 victory are worth the admission money by themselves.

4 DECEMBER: A 2–1 defeat in Auxerre. Gough scores his last European goal.

10 DECEMBER: A bizarre mix-up betwen Goram and Gough leads to a goal and a 1–0 Dundee United win.

2 JANUARY: The Nine-in-a-row pressure is showing all over Glasgow; and in an astonishing match, Albertz scores a brilliant free kick, Di Canio equalizes, Andersen comes on for a quickfire double, Walter Smith celebrates with a run up the touchline and Cadete has a goal ruled off. Another test of character is passed.

16 JANUARY: Disaster in a seven-a-side tournament as Ajax 'keeper Fred Grimm commits a ludicrous foul on Gascoigne, who will be out until after Easter.

18 JANUARY: £3.5 million Sebastian Rozental's debut at Motherwell is a 3–1 win.

25 JANUARY: Rozental's first goal – and, unbelievably, a debilitating knee injury too.

1 MARCH: Rangers draw 2–2 at Aberdeen thanks to Moore and Laudrup, but Goram's mistake hints at the problems he is about to encounter. A 15-match unbeaten run culminates this day.

6 MARCH: Celtic rise to the Scottish Cup challenge, Rangers don't. Goram's injury doesn't help, as he must play with a pain-killing injection. A 2–0 defeat.

12 MARCH: Stricken by injury and form problems at exactly the wrong time, Rangers are blown away by Dundee United at Ibrox 0–2.

16 MARCH: In an afternoon to match the Aberdeen win of May 1991, Rangers display incredible commitment and attitude. Hateley jumps, Durrant chases and lobs the ball, Laudrup and Mackay end up in the net. Laudrup's touch – but spiritually Durrant's goal? In any case, it is the one that wins the League.

22 MARCH: Doing it the hard way, Rangers go down 1–2 at home to eventual Scottish Cup winners Kilmarnock. Durie is the scorer.

15 APRIL: Gascoigne returns – and makes a goal. Rangers win 6–0 at Raith. Surely, now … ?

5 MAY: Motherwell want three points more than some Rangers players seem to want Nine-in-a-row. Gough's last Ibrox match ends 0–2.

7 MAY: It is so fitting that Laudrup scores the winning goal of the ninth championship. Dundee United are beaten 0–1: Gazza refuses to be substituted. There is a jubilant huddle in the middle of the pitch which suddenly finds Walter Smith landing on top of it. Nine-in-a-row.

5 JULY: Gascoigne re-negotiates his contract to stay until the year 2000.

It started on the road and that's where it was won. History is made again at Tannadice, 7 July 1997

Chapter 3
Rangers in Europe

In recent seasons, Rangers fans have been divided on the European issue. Although none would actually have spurned progression in the Champions' League, the pressing desire to equal and beat Celtic's long-standing record became all-consuming for most – particularly the Euro-sceptics.

But however much the support has changed in recent years, there will always be those who remember that Rangers were true European aristocrats. That was the golden era, when in their first 15 years of UEFA competition they contested three finals, two semi-finals and two quarter-finals. It was a record which marked them out amongst the elite even then, but which today would earn them well over £100 million if such success were replicated in the Champions' League.

The night of supreme achievement came in Barcelona on 24 May 1972, when Rangers beat Dynamo Moscow 3–2 to lift the European Cup-winners' Cup. It was a marvellous performance, the climax to a series of superb victories through the rounds, which was somewhat darkened by the subsequent extra time played out between General Franco's over-zealous police and the Rangers' fans on the pitch.

The inexhaustible hunger for European trophies which English football developed in the 1970s and early 1980s has helped overshadow Rangers' initial achievements. Indeed, its current profile as a big name in European competition is based on the fact that only four times since its debut has the club failed to qualify for that stage.

But always being at the party is not the same thing as being the belle of the ball. There has been no true success in the last two decades, during which time both Aberdeen and Dundee United made it to the semi-finals and finals of the European Cup and the Cup-winners' Cup.

The glorious exception was in the 1992–93 season when a stirringly resolute Rangers team came within an ace of the European Cup final, only to be held off by the talented but subsequently tainted and discredited Marseilles side, whose record of bribery only emerged when it was far too late for Rangers to replace them in the latter stages. With the advent of increasing ticket prices and less-competitive sides in the last couple of seasons, there have been facile questions about how much the Ibrox public truly desire the big European nights.

But the catalyst for moving back to the future will be David Murray. He knows that football's moneymen became Europhiles some time ago and Rangers must make up ground extremely quickly, and then continue to perform consistently at the highest level, if they are not to be devastated – both economically and in football terms.

The 1996–97 season saw investments of £40 million by billionaire Joe Lewis, attracted because he sees Rangers as a lucrative return on his money, and 1997–98 brought Lorenzo Amoruso, Stale Stensaas, Jonas Thern, Sergio Porrini, Rino Gattuso and Marco Negri – all purchased to add top-level edge to Rangers' future Continental excursions.

These are exciting times. It is widely believed that UEFA wants its millennium project to be an extensive, mid-week, pan-Continental league. Rangers have but three seasons to muscle their way closer to the top table, and Murray has clearly made that objective his marker of success or failure from now on.

Early successes: 1956–67

The European Cup was born only because Gabriel Hanot, the visionary football correspondent of France's *L'Equipe* sports newspaper, had both the desire to see an international competition and the sheer stubbornness not to let the subject drop.

When finally, in April 1955, it was agreed that "The Champions' Cup" should go ahead, Rangers kept a close eye on the success of Hibs, who reached the semi-final of the first tournament, and decided that they didn't like being left out. So they won the League.

Not having bothered with a foreign match for six years, they set off in May 1956 and prepared for what lay ahead by playing Mahon, Barcelona and Valencia (three times) in the space of a fortnight. However, nothing could really have prepared them for what was waiting in their European debut against OGC Nice in the autumn.

Rangers won an Ibrox roughhouse 2–1 when English referee Arthur Ellis mistakenly halted the game with several minutes left, discovered his mistake and then called the players back – including poor old Eric Caldow, who was already soaking his bruises in the bath.

Rangers lost the return 2–1 when Nice's Bravo and Rangers' Willie Logie were sent off, resulting in the referee requiring a police escort off the pitch.

In the Parc des Princes replay, Rangers were beaten 3–1 in another remarkable 90 minutes which saw Muro carted off on a stretcher and Bruno and Shearer

Iain Durrant's goal against Ajax in 1990 was a consolation but the player seems to thrive in Europe

"sent off", according to the referee's report – though, confusingly, both were allowed to complete the game.

By May 1960 the club had reached the first of its European semi-finals: the Champions' Cup against Eintracht Frankfurt. Having gone out in the first round of their initial competition and been humbled by AC Milan the following year (Rangers led 1–0 at Ibrox before conceding four goals in just over 10 minutes to the Italians) the club then failed to qualify for Europe at all in the 1958–59 season – hardly the most auspicious start. But they stormed into the new decade, going through the rounds by scoring seven times against Anderlecht, then beating Red Star Belgrade and Sparta Rotterdam.

What was waiting was nothing more than a cruel mismatch. Eintracht Frankfurt were playing a different game altogether, tactically, technically and athletically, which accounts for their aggregate 12–4 win. The brilliance of the football displayed in their 6–3 rout at Ibrox partly accounts for the 134,000-strong crowd a few weeks later at Hampden to watch that classic European Cup final when Frankfurt themselves found a peerless rival outclassing them, as Real Madrid thrashed the Germans 7–3.

Inspired, Rangers extended themselves and the next season reached the final of the inaugural Cup-winners' Cup, which was also notable for the debut of one of the club's most revered players of all time – Jim Baxter. As it was, Rangers' progress to the final was devastating. Revenge was taken for that Eintracht Frankfurt debâcle when Borussia Mönchengladbach were hammered 11–0 on aggregate.

There had been much ill-feeling following the first leg in Germany, when Rangers won 3–0 but Borussia had to face widespread accusations of bad sportsmanship and violent tactics: all in all, the perfect build-up to a warm Ibrox welcome.

Rare though it became, Rangers simply toyed with their German opponents, scoring almost at will, out-passing, out-playing and out-thinking them. Brand became the first Rangers player to score a hat-trick in European competition but McMillan was the best player in both matches, repeatedly teasing the Borussia defenders into rash, diving tackles.

One commentator, seeing the centre-half Gobbels wearing the Number 12 shirt in the second half, dryly remarked that "if Borussia had brought numbers 13, 14, 15 and 16 on they would still have been a poor second-best".

Better still – or so the 80,000 at Ibrox on 29 March 1961 thought – England's FA Cup-winners, Wolves, were beaten 2–0 and then held 1–1 three weeks later for a 3–1 aggregate and an open door to the final. There Fiorentina were a better side than the Scots, but Rangers were authors of their own demise at Ibrox.

Defensive slackness gave away the first and Eric Caldow then unusually missed a penalty before Milan hit his second to give the Florentines a lead which was not to be challenged. At least Alex Scott scored in the second-leg 2–1 defeat, but a first chance for European glory came, went and was not to be offered again for the next 11 years.

Still, there was a certain momentum to Rangers' assault on the Continent: in 1961–62 they were to ascend to the quarter-final, where Standard Liège of Belgium were comfortable home winners 4–1, but through Ralph Brand and Eric Caldow Rangers took the second leg to 4–3 on aggregate – as close as they were to get.

Interestingly, winger Willie Henderson simply arrived too late for the Ibrox match to be included in the starting line-up, but on the plus side an 18-year-old John Greig made his European debut in the first leg – one of 857 appearances for the club.

Thrashings from Spurs in 1962 and then the imperious Real Madrid the following year, plus defeat in the British Cup by Everton, hinted at a lack of quality, but in fact the team was merely maturing, and two vintage campaigns followed.

The first was in 1964–65, when the prolific Jim Forrest scored 57 goals in 50 matches; yet Rangers

---

FAMOUS MATCHES IN EUROPE

Rangers vs. Borussia Mönchengladbach

European Cup-winners' Cup, Second Round

30 November 1960

Venue: Ibrox Stadium, Glasgow

Attendance: 38,174
HT 5–0, FT 8–0

Scorers: Baxter, Brand (3), Pfeiffer (og), Millar (2), Davis.

Rangers:
Niven, Shearer, Caldow, Davis, Paterson, Baxter, Scott, McMillan, Millar, Brand, Wilson.

Borussia Mönchengladbach:
Jansen G, De Lange, Gobbels, Pfeiffer, Frentzek, Jansen A, Brungs, Brulls, Kohn, Mulhausen, Fendel.

were so far off the domestic pace, winning nothing, that he might as well not have bothered. They did, however contest the Champions' Cup quarter-final against holders Internazionale of Milan. Two strong opponents were beaten – Red Star Belgrade and Rapid Vienna – but at a cost. Jim Baxter was crudely challenged in a last-minute tackle which broke his leg and, according to all those who knew him at his peak, affected his subsequent career. Until that point, he had given one of the finest individual performances of any Rangers' player in Europe, and it was genuinely sad that he was not to pit his skills against Helenio Herrera's Italian champions.

Rangers lost three goals in three minutes in front of 50,000 fanatical fans in the San Siro. Forrest, of course, got one back and in the second leg he scored again, setting up one of the archetypal Scottish nights in Europe. The Scots gave a pulsating display of their own game but the defensive chastity-belt which Herrera himself had invented was simply locked and the key thrown away.

Rangers failed to qualify for Europe that year but, as before, missing out simply made Rangers ensure that they were a little more "Aye Ready" the next time. In fact 1966–67 was the year when Glasgow became European football's premier city. Rangers had been pipped by Celtic in every trophy bar the Scottish Cup, when it was Berwick Rangers: then, seven days before Rangers played Bayern Munich in their own final, Celtic beat Inter 2–1 to become the first British club to win the Champions' Cup.

There is no doubt that the whole effect cast something of a cloud over Rangers' approach to the final, which is unfair given the mature European performance they had produced against the holders Borussia Dortmund to make it that far. Taking a 2–1 lead to Germany, Rangers had to earn their 0–0 draw by defending with 10 men for 50 minutes after Bobby Watson was carried off. John Greig then won a toss-of-the-coin decider against Real Zaragoza in Spain when the quarter-final ended 2–2 on aggregate.

Munich in the final was a daunting prospect. Although Sepp Maier, Gerd Muller and Franz Beckenbauer were not then as feared as they later became, Munich was still powered by some of the exceptional talents of the last 30 years and the venue, Nuremburg, was close enough for tens of thousands of Bavarians to swamp the stadium.

Against Munich, Rangers bizarrely used a defender up-front instead of striker Alex Willoughby, and their performance was flat and uninspiring, reflecting the fact that the Scottish domestic season had been over for weeks. The Germans scored in the first half of extra time for a 1–0 victory so Rangers' time had not come; but it would.

Victory, then decline: 1968–85

Two subsequent seasons in the Inter-City Fairs Cup brought nothing more than successive defeats from English clubs, although Rangers went out in the quarter-final and the semi-final respectively.

The quarter-final of 1968 was notable for the 43,000 fans who watched the Elland Road leg live on closed-circuit television at Ibrox: Don Revie's side still won 2–0 thanks to John Giles and Peter Lorimer.

The semi-final of 1969 went the same way – 0–0 at Ibrox and a 2–0 defeat in England – but the Newcastle leg was badly scarred by crowd trouble, flying beer-bottles and a pitch invasion, the latter being held against Rangers when it happened again in 1972. Gornik Zabrze and Bayern Munich then eliminated Rangers in the following seasons.

But then came the Cup-Winners' Cup of 1971–72. This time they won it. So emotive was that night in Barcelona that it is largely forgotten that Rangers very nearly did not get there: in fact, they were "eliminated" in the second round thanks to the worst piece of officiating Rangers have experienced in 41 years of European football.

Rangers won the first leg 3–2 at Ibrox, and scored through Willie Henderson in extra time of the second leg to make the score 4–3 to Sporting Lisbon. That should have seen Rangers through on the away goals rule, but for quite some time everybody seemed to forget, and Lisbon won a penalty shoot-out.

Only when the UEFA observer managed to reach the Dutch referee Leo Horn, and Scottish football reporter John Fairgreave reached the Rangers dressing-room, were the false impressions corrected. Players were already half-stripped, dejection had set in and Rangers, for a mercifully short time, had been out of the Cup.

Instead they went on to beat Torino 2–1 and Bayern Munich 3–1 to land in the Barcelona final against Moscow Dynamo. Five minutes after half-time Rangers were 3–0 up and had cut the Russians wide open, with superb passes from Dave Smith enabling Colin Stein and Willie Johnston to score, Johnston then adding the third.

But Rangers' last competitive game had been over three weeks previously, and John Greig had been out injured since the Scottish Cup semi-final on 15 April. Exhausted, they almost crumbled, Eschtrekov scoring with half an hour left and Mekovikov with three minutes left on the clock.

Although the subsequent reaction of the fans – dancing out their happiness on the pitch – was unquestionably against the rules, the Spanish police had allowed the same thing to happen before the match and the mix of cheap beer, sangria and victory was always bound to lead to a repeat.

FAMOUS MATCHES IN EUROPE

Rangers vs. Dynamo Moscow

European Cup-Winners' Cup Final

24 May 1972
Venue: Nou Camp, Barcelona

Attendance: 45,000
HT 2–0, FT 3–2

Scorers Rangers: Stein, Johnston (2).
Scorers Moscow: Eschtrekov, Mekovikov.

Rangers:
McCloy, Jardine, Mathieson, Greig, Johnstone, Smith, McLean, Conn, Stein, McDonald, Johnston.

Dynamo Moscow:
Pilgul, Basalcev, Dolmatov, Zsykov, Dolbonossov, Jukov, Baidachnyi, Jakubik, Sabo, Mahovikov, Evrizhikin.

Roared on by at least 30,000 ecstatic fans draped in blue, Rangers blew the Russians away for close to an hour and were 3–0 up before legs and lungs gave way. Greig's five-week absence with an injury made his performance almost miraculous; but it was Stein, with a vicious drive and his assistance with Johnston's second goal, who tilted the balance.

Dave Smith's clinical passes made the first two goals and, by the end, McCloy had emerged as a defiant goalkeeper. The end was mayhem, with Mekovikov adding to Eschtrekov's earlier goal, Smith kicking off the line and a pitch invasion just before and just after the final whistle.

The consequences were serious. Rangers received a two-year ban from European football and therefore never defended their crown. John Greig never enjoyed that moment of lifting a European trophy above his head while adoring fans gave rapturous applause, something he still calls "the biggest anti-climax of my life". He was handed the trophy in the dressing-room.

What has never been dimmed is the glorious nature of the win. Five excellent clubs were defeated and Rangers remain the only Scottish club to score three times in a European final. Strangely, and sadly, it marked the start of a slow, continuous decline. The ban was cut to one year, but not for seven seasons did Rangers even reached the quarters again. The real low point was undoubtedly Rangers' first-ever defeat in Europe by a Swiss side – Zurich – in 1976.

Jock Wallace had taken over from Willie Waddell shortly after the 1972 triumph but his own European debut, the 6–3 defeat by Ajax in the Rangers' first European Super Cup, was a foretaste of his fortunes on the Continent. Not until John Greig succeeded him in 1978 did Rangers have anything to enjoy in Europe.

Realistically, 1978–79 should have been a brief, miserable affair in the Champions' Cup as Rangers drew Juventus, starring nine players from Italy's World Cup semi-final squad of barely two months earlier – notably Roberto Bettega, Dino Zoff, Franco Causio and Marco Tardelli.

Stein's classy finish opens the floodgates against Moscow Dynamo in the 1972 Cup-Winners' Cup

Victory, then decline 1968–85

Although it is not the Camp Nou Stadium, parading the Cup-Winners' Cup is a glorious moment

Having lost 1–0 in Turin, Rangers overcame the fact that they had never overturned a first-leg defeat in a night of superb football and unforgettable noise. Goals from Alex MacDonald and Gordon Smith saw Rangers through to a wonderful contest in Holland against PSV Eindhoven. The Dutch, too, were replete with World Cup stars, having made the final, but Rangers overcame a 0–0 home draw to give PSV their first-ever European home defeat.

No one who was at the Juventus match could be easily persuaded that Rangers have ever pulled off a better European performance. Not having won a single game in the League to date, Rangers left Juventus beaten, dishevelled and hoisting the white flag long before the end. New manager John Greig produced the winning tactical switch, moving Tommy McLean from right to left wing and using the ever-dependable Sandy Jardine at sweeper.

Nine of the Italians had been good enough for the World Cup semi-final stage a few weeks earlier, but goals from MacDonald and Smith turfed them out of the European Cup. Afterwards Greig said: "It was great to see such a professional side as Juventus reduced to such chaos".

FAMOUS MATCHES IN EUROPE

Rangers vs. Juventus

European Cup First Round

27 September 1978

Venue: Ibrox Stadium, Glasgow

Attendance: 44,000
HT 1–0, FT 2–0

Scorers Rangers: McDonald, Smith.

Rangers:
McCloy, Jardine, A Forsyth, T Forsyth, Jackson, McDonald, McLean, Russell, Parlane, Johnstone, Smith.

Juventus:
Zoff, Cuccureddu, Cabrini, Furino, Morini, Scirea, Causio, Tardelli, Virdis, Gentile, Bettega.

Against PSV, with all due respect to goals from Alex McDonald and Derek Johnstone, the sublime moment was Bobby Russell's. With three minutes left, Rangers built from their own box and Tommy McLean laid an exquisite pass on to the break from Russell, who curved the ball home around the advancing 'keeper. Rangers' third side was an international-packed Cologne in the quarters, and the Germans, with goals from German centre-forward Dieter Muller in each leg, went through 2–1.

A further eight years of early defeats by the likes of Dukla Prague, Valencia, Cologne, Porto, Inter and then Osasuna passed before Rangers reached the last eight again, the miserable interim paving the way for Graeme Souness's astounding arrival from Sampdoria.

The Grand Obsession: 1985–97

Souness understandably found it easier to impact at speed in Scotland than in Europe, and won the title in his first full season. But while doing so, Rangers went out on away goals to Borussia Mönchengladbach in the third round of the UEFA Cup.

Rangers' only match in Europe where the touch-lines were more famous than the players

In 1987–88 an exhilarating performance at Ibrox put Dynamo Kiev out 2–1, winning worldwide attention because Souness had ordered the touchlines to be moved inward to restrict the playing area. It caused some Ukranian spluttering, but Rangers went on. Steau Bucharest proved too much in the quarter-final, after winning 2–0 in Romania: Marius Lacatus stole an early goal at Ibrox but at least Rangers re-grouped and 4won the home leg 2–1.

It was as far as Souness's personal revolution at Ibrox was to take him in European competition, as Rangers were outclassed by good Cologne, Bayern Munich and Red Star Belgrade teams in consecutive years. Belgrade, in particular, were a wonderful side and Walter Smith, in his first season, was unfortunate to draw an equally-talented Eastern European opponent in Sparta Prague. But Smith might have had an early triumph from the aggregate 2–1 lead in extra time at Ibrox had not a combined cock-up by Scott Nisbet and Andy Goram gifted that vital away goal which always seems to haunt Scottish sides.

Then came the heart-stopping excitement of 1992–93 – Rangers' finest European performances for 20 years. Two qualifying rounds were needed to get to the group stage from which a finalist would emerge. Lyngby were comprehensively beaten 3–0 to set up a match with Leeds which was hyped to the heavens as "The Battle of Britain". Gary McAllister's brilliant early goal at Ibrox tilted the odds, but Rangers then went on to score four times over the two matches before Leeds did so again.

The Elland Road victory, marvellous in itself, put Rangers in a group with Brugges, CSKA Moscow and

---

FAMOUS MATCHES IN EUROPE

Leeds United vs. Rangers

Champions' League Qualifier

4 November 1992

Venue: Elland Road, Leeds

Attendance: 25,118
HT 0–1, FT 1–2

Scorers Rangers: Hateley, McCoist.
Scorers Leeds: Cantona.

Rangers:
Goram, McCall, Robertson, Gough, McPherson, Brown, Durran, McCoist, Hateley, Gordon, Ferguson

Leeds:
Lukic, Newsome, Dorigo, Rocastle, Fairclough, Whyte, Strachan, Cantona, Chapman, McAllister, Speed.

McCoist's goal at Elland Road to put Rangers in the Champions' League was one of the best of his career

Marseilles – the first British club to play in the Champions' League. It was to prove a Champions' Cup effort to be proud of, and a place in the final against Milan did not completely slip away until the second half of the last group match against Moscow.

The fact that Rangers became the first British club in the Champions' League and the only British club left in Europe with this victory was less important than winning the "Battle of Britain". Hateley may never have scored a finer goal than the one which fizzed over Lukic from 25 yards after less than three minutes, and then his cross for McCoist to score the winner was par excellence.

It was McCoist's 29th goal of the season, in only November, and when Leeds tried to preserve their 30-match undefeated run, Goram excelled in keeping Cantona out until minutes from time, when he eventually scored from close in. It was the thrilling gateway to a barnstorming campaign.

A draw and a win against the Russians and against Brugge were creditable results, much to be coveted by subsequent Rangers sides. But the two draws against Marseilles were monumental affairs. The first group match opened with the French outplaying an inexperienced Ibrox side to a hideous degree. Goram was besieged, Rudi Voller and Alen Boksic both scored. With minutes remaining and the score 2–0, young Gary McSwegan came on as a substitute and headed a lovely goal; then Hateley barnstormed an equalizer with little time left.

In the Velodrome, Rangers were again put through the wringer after Sauzee's early goal and further heroics from Goram. But Durrant hit a wonderful curving shot from outside the box and a point was gained.

Hateley brings the house down with the equalizer against Marseille in the 1992 Champions' League

The last match was a 0–0 draw with Moscow, despite incredible chances, which meant that Marseilles, who won against Brugge, were through. But given the Frenchmen's subsequent match-rigging trials theirs was a dark triumph, and Rangers are entitled to wonder about the tame defeats to which both the Belgians and Russians succumbed.

The next season, an agonising last-minute thunderbolt from Levski Sofia's Todorov put Rangers out in the first round on the away goals rule. After 10 unbeaten games the previous campaign, and so close to the final, it was a sickening blow – equalled in 1994–95 by AEK Athens's 3–0 aggregate victory in the qualifying round of the Champions' League. But defeats of Anorthosis from Cyprus and Russia's Alania Vladikavkaz in the 1995–96 and 1996–97 seasons have meant 12 lucrative matches in the latter stages, with tens of millions earned.

Nevertheless, those games have been a watershed period, with only one win, three draws and eight defeats. Setting aside the aggregate 8–1 and 5–1 defeats inflicted on Juventus and Ajax, Rangers will be concentrating their attention on the narrow line separating a draw from a defeat against Steau Bucharest, Borussia Dortmund and Auxerre.

Immediately after sifting through the lessons of the 1996–97 Champions' League campaign, Walter Smith abandoned his preference for a predominantly

Rangers' thrashing of Russian champions Alania Vladikavkaz was as enjoyable as it was surprising

Gordon Durie in action for Rangers against Italian giants Juventus during the 1995–96 campaign

Scottish team and David Murray funded the purchase of Porrini, Amoruso, Negri, Rozental and Stensaas, and the wages of Thern and Vidmar.

Smith has inherited conditions which make European competition difficult: no world-class or even European-class Scots available to buy or even being produced; a sadly poor standard of Scottish football which hinders the buying of world-class foreigners; and continental competition which is moving ahead both tactically and technically as the Scots can only watch.

Never in their history have Rangers faced such a challenge in Europe: but never before has the club turned its attention so single-mindedly towards the vast earnings potential of the Champions' League and whatever European League is to follow it.

Chapter 4
Up for the Cup

Over the years, the domestic cups in Scotland have provided Rangers with equal amounts of joy and pain. From defeat against Berwick to glory against Celtic, the love affair with the cup continues in the 1990s

Although Rangers are believed to have been one of the founding clubs which chipped in to buy the actual "Scotch Cup" in 1873, when a whip-round of all the registered SFA members was taken to raise the price of £56 12s. 11d., the love-affair between investor and trophy has been a somewhat stormy one.

Protests, riots, abandonments, countless sunny Saturday afternoons at Hampden Park in front of jubilant six-figure crowds, so many tussles with Celtic and that incredible defeat by Berwick – the Scottish Cup will always hold a special fascination for Rangers. But the trophy has taunted Rangers with long barren spells in their pursuit of it – something of which its less prestigious sister, the Scottish League Cup, is not so guilty.

In a country whose football hinges so completely on the Old Firm, it is even more inevitable that the League title is the ultimate prize – one often competed for by the two Glasgow clubs in first and second place. But that has always left the cup competitions as a particularly vital battleground for the side which is failing in the League – a chance to beat the other in the final, eliminate it in an early round or win it if the other has already been knocked out.

Add to that the spice of European competition being guaranteed in late autumn for a League Cup win, or the Cup-Winners' Cup for a Scottish Cup victory, and the importance of each competition to the coffers and egos of Rangers and Celtic becomes crystal-clear.

The Scottish Cup has been lifted on 27 occasions by a Rangers captain, significantly less often than the 47 championships won over an almost identical length of time, while the League Cup has been brought to Ibrox 20 times – more than any other club in Scotland.

For several Rangers managers – to be precise, for Bill Struth, Scot Symon, Jock Wallace and Walter Smith – a Scottish Cup victory has also meant that the team they have put together, worked with, sweated over and cursed at has managed to win the domestic treble of League Cup, League and Scottish Cup – heaven for any Rangers supporter.

That sunny day in May can send the team into the following season defending three titles, but it can also be dreadfully elusive – even a thorn in the side. Graeme Souness, for all the massive impact he had on the club, its signings, the support and its financial aspirations, never won the Cup.

His rampant era was stained by defeats at the hands of Hamilton and Dunfermline in early rounds, plus three losses to Celtic. But these frustrations were all the more incomprehensible in that his teams won four League Cups in five seasons: winning knock-out competitions was nothing – only the Scottish Cup counted.

Finisher and provider: Durie scored the hat-trick but Laudrup was the inspiration behind the goals

The trio of League Cup finals from 1987–89, all against Aberdeen, will always be remembered as a little cluster of classic matches; but it is predominantly in the Scottish Cup, over three-quarters of a century older than the newcomer, that historic events take place.

The riots of 1909 and 1980 are a blemish on the game, but the latter at least led to the prohibition of alcohol at Scottish football matches.

Rangers' 1928 win against Celtic, after a quarter of a century without the trophy, will always remain a cherished result in the history of the club, as will its monumental triumph in the Centenary Cup final – another classic way to end a barren spell.

But how to separate that from the dominant times? Twice in the last 20 years Rangers have beaten Aberdeen 2–1 on the last day of the season to lift the Cup and win the treble – each time in the blazing sunshine, with nothing but a summer of gloating to look forward to.

Above all, however, Rangers fans will never lose a sense of investment in the Scottish Cup – the competition which brought them the opportunity to win their one and only European trophy so far, the Cup-Winners' Cup in 1972.

From Wilton to Wallace

Rangers' love-hate relationship with the Scottish Cup started before either club or competition had reached its teens, so perhaps the incident can be understood as an outbreak of childishness on both sides.

Vale of Leven had already beaten Rangers 3–2 in the 1877 Cup Final, after two 1–1 draws, and then put them out of the next season's quarter-final 5–0 after a 0–0 draw. It is not stretching credulity too much to suggest that there was an extra competitive edge to the final of 1879, when the two sides met once again.

There was a crowd of just under 10,000 at Hampden for the final, and Rangers opened with their leading scorer of the time, Willie Struthers, before seeming to score again when he headed in. But the goal was disallowed, and Vale equalized late on. Rangers lodged an official complaint to the SFA "protesting against the decision of umpires and referee respecting a second goal which was taken by Rangers but disallowed on the unanimous decision of both umpires". The protest was rejected, as was the appeal, but Rangers remained aggrieved and simply did not turn up for the replay on 26 April when Vale trotted unopposed up the pitch to score and win the Cup.

Seven years later, Rangers were 3–0 up against Arbroath before crumbling to 4–3 and then measuring the pitch, which they found to be too small. The SFA received a telegram from Rangers saying "Beaten on a backyard": initially the protest made no difference, but then Arbroath were made to change their pitch and Rangers won the re-match at Ibrox 8–1.

It took 21 years of trying for Rangers to win the Cup, but when it came the victory was against arch-rivals Celtic, making it sweeter still. It was the first Old Firm final ever and Rangers, through McReadie, Barker and McPherson, won 3–1 against a Celtic side which dealt less well with the foul conditions.

Twice in the next fifteen years there were to be much more combustible meetings. In the semi-final of 1905 at Parkhead, a weakened Rangers team went 0–2 ahead before Celtic's Jimmy Quinn was sent off for violence. Some fans invaded the pitch and refused to leave until the game was abandoned. Rangers were later awarded the match but lost the final 3–1 to Third Lanark.

Bad blood surfaced again in 1909 – and in a big way. The League match of a month earlier had merited an SFA inquiry because of violent play, and the Cup Final was surrounded by continual allegations from fans that draws were deliberately played for in order to increase gate revenue from replays.

Sure enough, Rangers were leading 2–1 when goalkeeper Harry Rennie carried the ball over his line in order to avoid the charging Jimmy Quinn. Referee Stark gave a goal, and controversy raged until the replay. 60,000 turned out for the second match: once again, it ended in a draw, and as the players were leaving the pitch the crowd cried "Play on" – demanding extra time, not yet another replay. A policeman and a demonstrator clashed and the crowd rioted. Posts were ripped out and paraded around, wooden barricades torn up, bonfires made and mounted police charges repelled by fans stoning them from the terraces. Fire-engines were called but their hoses were cut; and not until 300 police reinforcements were called to augment the original 97 was peace restored. No replay was called for and the Cup was withheld.

Earlier, in 1903, Rangers had beaten Hearts 2–0 in the final to win their fourth Scottish Cup – little suspecting it would be 25 years before they won another. By that time Willie Wilton had died and Bill Struth was in charge.

Not a meeting of Chicago Hoods, but the Rangers' heroes who won the cup in 1928 after a 25 year wait

The 1928 final was a momentous game which Rangers won 4–0 against Celtic. But almost as importantly as ending the drought, the victory which Dave Meiklejohn inspired immediately unlocked Rangers' ability to punch their weight in the Cup

> **SCOTTISH CUP FINAL**
>
> **18 April 1928**
> Venue: Hampden Park
>
> **Ranger 4**
> Meiklejohn, McPhail, Archibald (2)
>
> **Celtic 0**
>
> HT 0–0 FT 4–0
> Att: 118,115
>
> **Rangers:**
> T Hamilton, Gray, R Hamilton, Buchanan, Meiklejohn, Craig, Archibald, Cunningham, Fleming, McPhail, Morton
>
> **Celtic:**
> J Thomson, McStay, Donoghue, Wilson, J McStay, McFarlane, Connolly, A Thomson, McGrory, McInally, McLean

It was won in 1930 against Thistle, in 1932 with a victory over Kilmarnock, in 1934 by 5–0 against St Mirren, in 1935 against Hamilton and again in 1936 to complete the hat-trick, Rangers' first, against Third Lanark in the final

So dominant were Rangers in the inter-war period that their 25-year failure to win the Scottish Cup ceased to be questioned or analyzed and simply became the easiest music-hall joke in the business. Even in 1921, when Rangers had only lost to Celtic all season in a record-breaking championship win, they had contrived to lose to Partick Thistle in the final on a day when the bookies had stopped taking bets on Rangers.

Honours had been even this season, with the Old Firm clubs winning two matches each, but Rangers' march to the final had been devastating – six straight wins and 17 goals scored. Even so, Celtic almost opened the scoring with a shot from Paddy Connolly and Tom Hamilton had to produce an astoundingly athletic leap to block it. Then came the tumultous turning point to a quarter-century of failure. Alan Morton lobbed from the left and Fleming volleyed past Celtic keeper John Thomson, but McStay punched off the line – saving a goal but conceding a penalty. At that stage, Meiklejohn was neither first, second or any choice as penalty-taker, nor was he captain. But he shouldered everyone out of the way, closed his mind to 25 cupless years and smashed the ball past Thomson. His team-mates seemed to know that it was the turning point and they put Celtic to the sword: Bob McPhail scored just over 10 minutes later and two Archibald screamers from distance completed the highest Cup Final score for 20 years. And against Celtic into the bargain!

The war years put an end to the Scottish Cup for the duration, but Rangers won the inaugural Scottish League Cup in 1946–47.

It was a time of dominance for the club, and in 1948–49, under the guidance of Bill Struth, came the first-ever modern treble of the League, Scottish League Cup (beating Raith Rovers 2–0) and Scottish Cup (won against Clyde 4–1 in the final).

It was a feat which would have been repeated the following season but for a rare defeat by East Fife in the League Cup semi-final – ironically, the team against whom Rangers retained the Scottish Cup that same season. These were still the days of amazing attendance figures but even so, for that East Fife vs. Rangers Scottish Cup final to draw over 120,000 fans was remarkable. In fact, the 1947–48 semi-final, when the Hibs' Famous Five wrestled with Rangers' Iron Curtain defence, was watched by 143,570.

The Scottish Cup final of 1953, against Aberdeen, is memorable for the bravery of young Rangers keeper George Niven, playing in his first-ever Hampden final, who dived at the feet of Aberdeen's free-scoring Paddy Buckley. Niven was stretchered off, but chose to return 20 minutes later wearing a rugby-style scrum cap as protection, and Rangers won 1–0. Again, it was one of those unnoticed moments when success seems commonplace but is about to vanish.

Rangers won neither cup competition between April 1953 and April 1960: a nasty seven-year itch. Worse still, the transition from Struth to Scot Symon also brought latter-stage defeats by Aberdeen (6–0) and Hearts (4–0) which should have been inconceivable given Rangers' ability to keep on winning the title. Then came – horror of horrors – a 7–1 record defeat by Celtic in the League Cup final of 1957–58.

So when the Scottish Cup Final of 1960 came along, thanks to a 4–1 semi final win over Celtic, Symon needed a win over Kilmarnock. Rangers had not actually lost a Cup final since 1929, but that had been preceded by 25 years without a victory and this seven-

Davie Wilson wheels away after scoring against St Mirren to win the 1962 Scottish Cup Final

year stretch was making the directors jittery.

Ian McColl was Man of the Match, despite Jimmy Millar's two goals in front of 108,000 fans, and Rangers had the Cup again. The very next season brought the League Cup for the first time since 1948–49 – again a resounding 2–0 win over Killy.

As often occurs in Rangers' trophy-festooned history, one win begets another and in 1961–62 both cups were won – the Scottish Cup 2–0 against St Mirren, and the League Cup 3–1 in a replay against Hearts, which was largely inspired by Baxter.

Important victories though all of these were, they were rather ordinary games - especially when viewed in the context of 125 years of history. But 1963 was a bit special, as May turned up the first Old Firm final for 35 years – since the 1928 final when Rangers ended their hoodoo in the Cup.

The first match produced one of those "unbeatable" afternoons from a goalkeeper, Frank Haffey of Celtic, but Rangers were a far superior side and the replay was a 3–0 thrashing which emptied the Celtic terraces long before the end. It was Part Two of the double that year.

Once more, that set Rangers off. They won the Scottish Cup and League Cup in 1963–64, beating Celtic three times and 8–0 on aggregate in the process.

The following two seasons brought the League Cup (2–1 against Celtic) and the Scottish Cup, 1–0 against Celtic thanks to a Kai Johansen goal. But these were just a prelude to disaster. No one who has anything to do with Rangers will ever forget the impact which Berwick Rangers' infamous victory in 1967 had on the club.

It was the cue for four years without trophies of any kind, but the thought of Berwick Rangers – even marshalled by Jock Wallace in goal – beating Rangers

Bobbie Shearer shows off the 1963 Cup as the delighted Rangers' fans dance a jig of delight

was as fanciful then as it is today. 27 January 1967 will never be forgotten – the first time Rangers had lost in the first round for 30 years and the first time this century that they had lost in the Cup to a club from a lower division.

The ignominy was worse still because, between 1966 and 1975, Rangers were reduced to aiming for Cup victories, so monotonous was Celtic's title-winning ability. Three Scottish Cup campaigns in a row between 1968–69 and 1970–71 ended at Celtic's hands, and it was a bleak time to be a Rangers fan. But it was the League Cup which provided succour, and Willie Waddell's first trophy when, in 1970–71, 16-year-old Derek Johnstone gave the club a 1–0 win over Celtic at Hampden in front of 106,263 fans.

In 1971 Rangers, and Willie Johnston in particular, squandered clear chances to win the Scottish Cup Final against Celtic; but reaching the final cleared the way for a shot at the Cup-Winners' Cup – already Rangers' favourite European competition.

1973 brought not only the centenary of the Scottish Cup but the end of another seven-year itch between victories in the competition for Rangers. The 3–2 win over Celtic was a gem of a match and the start of great things to come for the club. Willie Waddell turned out exactly the same team as in the first match, but in front of 54,435 instead of the 69,429 of five days earlier. Waddell's only change was to push Alfie Conn further forward to play closer to Colin Stein, a role which Alex McDonald had fulfilled in the first semi. Conn rewarded his manager with the winning goal after

Henderson had scored the opening Rangers' goal. In the end, the Gers were to lose the final 2–1 after a replay – to Celtic once again. But Celtic's victory in the title meant Jock Stein's team went into the European Cup and left Rangers in the Cup-Winners' Cup for the second consecutive season. No Rangers fan will need reminding that it was in this 1971–72 season that the club finally won the trophy after two previous appearances in the final. It may have seemed innocuous on the day, and worth very little once the final was lost to Celtic, but this semi-final victory over Hibernian was Rangers' passport into their greatest-ever triumph.

This was only a semi-final replay, but subsequent events in Europe make this one of the most, if not the most, significant Scottish Cup game Rangers have

16 year-old Derek Johnstone replaces flu victim John Greig and wins the 1971 League Cup

ever played. The first match between the two teams had been a fairly unexciting 0–0 draw, but Rangers had won the League Cup five months previously and desperately wanted to add the League Cup after a trophy drought stretching back to 1966.

SCOTTISH CUP SEMI-FINAL

5 April 1971
Venue: Hampden Park

Rangers 2
Henderson, Conn.

Hibernian 1
O'Rourke
HT 1–1 FT 2–1, Att: 54,435

Rangers:
McCloy, Jardine, Mathieson, Greig, McKinnon, Jackson, Henderson, McDonald, Stein, Conn, Johnston.

Hibernian:
Marshall, Brownlie, Jones, Blackley, Black, Pringle, Graham, O'Rourke, Baker, Cropley, Stevenson

This was the match in which the legend of Jock Wallace was born; when the first inkling was felt that Celtic's long domination of the domestic game might just be under threat; and Rangers' first Scottish Cup since a couple of weeks before England won the World Cup. It had been that long. The season had not been a vintage one in any way, with astonishing home defeats by second-division St Mirren 1–4 and Stenhousmuir 1–2. But 90 minutes of wonderful football were rolled out by the two teams and Rangers, at the end, were running Celtic ragged. Not normally a man for such emotions, John Greig was visibly in tears by the end and walked up to new manager Wallace saying, "You asked for the Cup: here it is", before thrusting the long-lost trophy to him. These were the days of phenomenal crowds and the warm May day brought a heaving, surging wall of noise as the game swung in either direction.

Dalglish's clean shot and Parlane's firm header left

SCOTTISH CUP FINAL

5 May 1973
Venue: Hampden Park

Rangers 3
Conn, Parlane, Forsyth

Celtic 2
Dalglish, Connelly (pen)

HT 1–1 FT 3–2
Att: 122,000

Rangers:
McCloy, Jardine, Mathieson, Greig, Johnstone, MacDonald, McLean, Forsyth, Parlane, Conn, Young. Sub: Smith

Celtic:
Hunter, McGrain, Brogan, Murdoch, McNeill, Connelly, Johnstone, Dalglish, Deans, Hay, Callaghan. Sub: Lennox

Alex McDonald in typical pose heads the winning goal for Rangers at Hampden in the 1976 League Cup

Miller and McCoist strain every sinew but it is Ally whose late strike wins Rangers the 1988 Skol Cup

the match at 1–1 as the second half was minutes old. But Conn sprinted away from McNeill and Brogan to push the ball under Hunter before Greig was forced to punch the ball off the line. George Connelly, so cool under pressure, made the penalty look deceptively simple and took the score to 2–2. But then Derek Johnstone, still only 18 but in his sixth major final, headed against the post and the ball trundled from left to right along the line, where Tom Forsyth stamped on it to score the most inelegant but most wildly-celebrated goal. A seven-year famine was over.

From Wallace to "Walter"

Jock Wallace is remembered with the greatest affection by all at Ibrox, and his funeral in the summer of 1996 was hugely well-attended. But 1973–74 passed without a trophy for Rangers, and although the title was won to huge acclaim in 1974–75, neither cup was captured that season. The next season, however, was Rangers' first treble since 1964. Alex McDonald's header beat Celtic in the League Cup Final and Rangers found Hearts easy going in the Scottish Cup, winning 3–1. 1976–77 was frustratingly free of a trophy once again, but the League Cup threw up an astonishing four-match sequence against Clydebank – three draws and a 2–1 win before progressing – which unearthed the legendary Davie Cooper, who signed for Rangers not long afterwards. But by 1977–78, Wallace turned up both Cups along with the League for his second treble. Celtic were beaten in the League Cup with a brilliant drive from Cooper and a Gordon Smith header after extra time, when Shug Edvaldsson had equalized. Then Bobby Russell turned in a virtuoso performance against Aberdeen in the Scottish Cup Final, although the goals came from Derek Johnstone and Alex McDonald headers.

Winning on that roasting-hot day in May 1978 was the last thing Wallace did for the club before resigning, and John Greig took over – leading Rangers to both cups the following season, against Celtic in the League Cup and Hibs in the Scottish. But by 1980 his team was playing poorly and expectations had been built up by Rangers reaching the Scottish Cup Final. A late George McCluskey winner sparked a pitch invasion and mini-riot, fuelled by drink, which led directly to legislation banning alcohol at football matches – a real turning-point in Scottish football history.

Greig's teams were thrown in the Cup, and despite winning the Scottish Cup and League Cup in 1981, both against Dundee United, lost successive Scottish Cup finals to Aberdeen in 1981–82 and 1982–83. The name of Ally McCoist eventually surfaced in March 1984 when Rangers, now under Jock Wallace again, beat Celtic 3–2 after extra time in a match when Coisty scored all his side's goals. Only seven months later, Ian Ferguson's solitary goal won Rangers their second League Cup final inside a calendar year – with United again the victims.

Then in 1986 came the Souness revolution. The title was his raison d'etre at Ibrox, and in that respect he was a success. But the Scottish Cup turned into one long unscratched itch for him. In fact Souness never laid hands on the Scottish Cup because his sides lost to Hamilton at home, to Dunfermline away, and then to Celtic on three separate occasions.

Hence there was a yawning, 11-year gap between Rangers' last victory, against Dundee United, and their 1991–92 Cup win over Airdrie, when Walter Smith ended the long and inexplicable run of misfortune. Smith's sides have subsequently won the Scottish Cup on two occasions – the brilliant season of 1992–93, ending in victory over Aberdeen, and the clinical destruction of Hearts in 1996 (see above). He has also continued Souness's pursuit of the League Cup with the 1996 classic against Hearts – two beautiful goals from Gascoigne in a 4–3 thriller at Parkhead – equalling the two superb finals of 1987 and 1988 against Aberdeen which respectively ended 3–3, with Rangers winning on penalties, and 3–2.

The campaign of 1995–96 had been a season of such hand-to-hand combat with the rejuvenated Celtic that when Tommy Burns's side were defeated 2–1 in the semi-final, some Rangers fans were expecting the final to be anticlimactic. But Hearts came to Hampden with a young, talented side which had actually taken five goals without reply from Rangers in their last two meetings. Moreover, it was Hearts who had put Rangers out of the Cup the previous season in a 4–2 fourth-round victory.

In the build-up to the match, Brian Laudrup warned: "If there is one team in Scotland I wouldn't like to go a goal behind to, it is Hearts. If they score first, it will be very difficult for us to win".

Some of his concern originated in the robust marking job Hearts' young captain Gary Locke had managed on Laudrup that season, but Locke departed in the first half with a bad injury and Rangers simply devastated the Edinburgh club.

Laudrup has rarely played so well and put Rangers in front with a run to collect Durie's pass and a volley from right to left across Gilles Rousset. Next he bamboozled the Frenchman into letting the ball slip underneath him, and then put a hat-trick on a plate for the jubilant Gordon Durie. Colquhoun's single reply was no more than a reward to Hearts' fans for their patience. It was as good a display as the final has seen in decades, and a brilliant way in which to win Rangers' 14th double.

Rangers also beat Celtic in the League Cups of 1986 and 1990, Aberdeen in 1992 and Hibs in 1993. Of these, the 1986 final brought Souness his first trophy at his first attempt, and featured the sending-off of Mo Johnston, subsequently signed by Souness to arouse such a furore. Such is the pressure on Rangers now in terms of fixtures and the lucrative nature of the European Cup that there is constant discussion of the merits of big clubs entering the competition later – or even abandoning it altogether. Future circumstances may demand such radical changes, but the League Cup has been the happiest of hunting grounds for Rangers over the years.

SCOTTISH CUP FINAL

18 May 1996
Venue: Hampden Park

Rangers 5
Laudrup (2) Durie (3)

Hearts 1
Colquhoun.

HT 1-0 FT 5-1
Att: 37,730

Rangers:
Goram, Cleland, Robertson, Gough, McLaren, Brown, Durie, Gascoigne, Ferguson (Durrant), McCall, Laudrup.

Hearts:
Rousset, Locke, Ritchie, McManus, McPherson, Bruno, Johnston, Mackay, Colquhoun, Fulton, Pointon.

Laudrup tormented Hearts in the 1996 Scottish Cup Final so Gazza did the same in the League Cup Final

From Wallace to "Walter" • 53

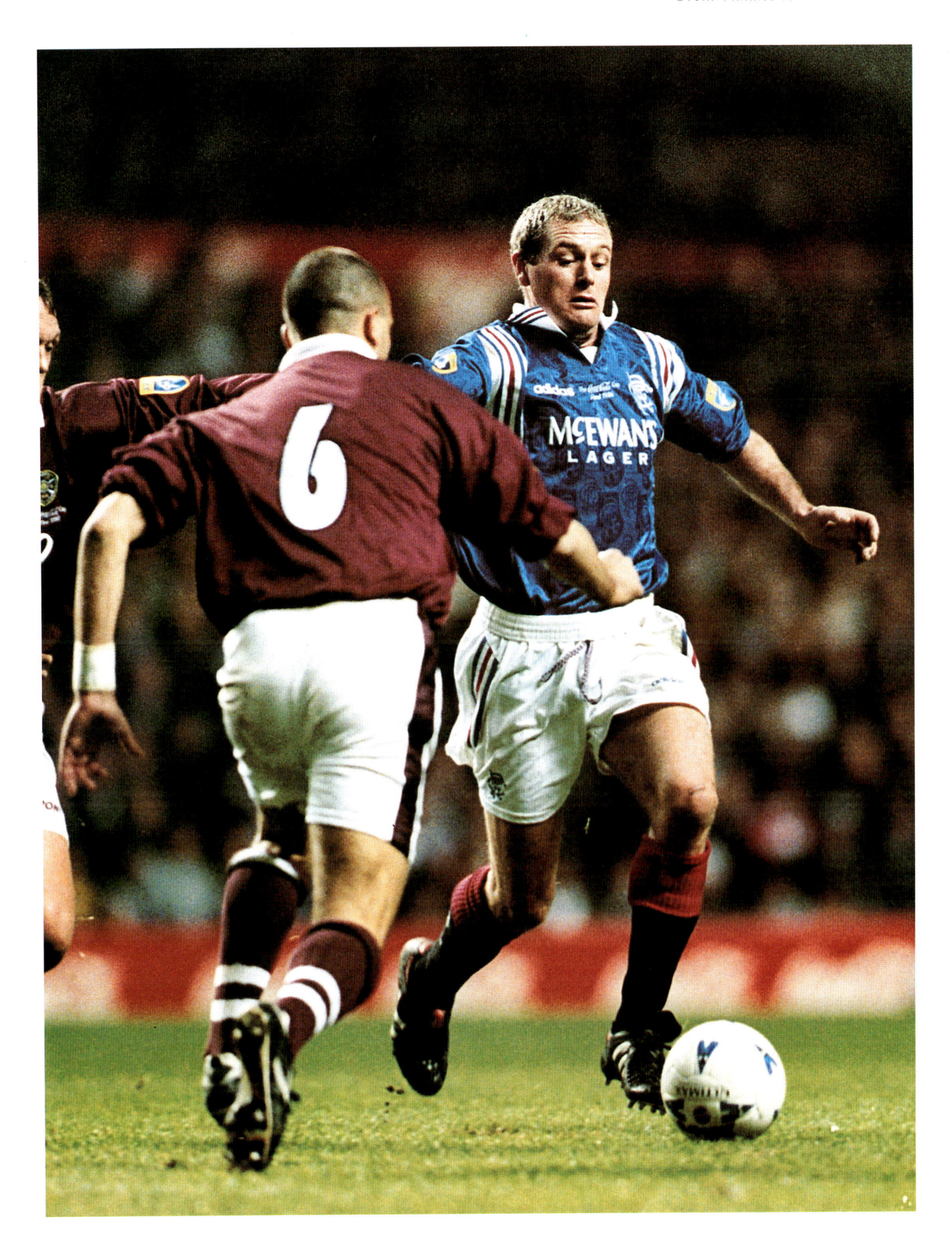

Chapter 5
Nine-in-a-Row Stars

While all the players involved in the nine titles have played their part, some have turned in some consistently outstanding performances

John Brown

John Brown epitomizes Rangers and is also one of the last of a very quickly dying breed – a top-class player who is, has always been and always will be a diehard supporter of the club he plays for. He has always been underrated – particularly on his technical ability and reading of the game. Clearly those who misjudge him are also unaware that he didn't become a full-time footballer until the age of 22 after having had both cartilages removed by the time he was 15.

When he signed for Graeme Souness in 1988, it was for the traditional reason of having played superbly against Rangers often enough. In fact, in 1985 he had scored to put them out of the Scottish Cup 1–0 and then followed that up, a few months later, with a hat-trick in a 3–2 win.

> **John BROWN**
> **Born:** 26 January 1962, Lennoxtown
> **Position:** Midfield
> **Height:** 5ft 11in
> **Weight:** 11st 2lb
> **Former clubs:** Hamilton Academicals, Dundee United
> **League appearances:** 185 (+21)
> **League goals:** 14

Brown was one of the real heroes of that massive performance on the last day of the 1990–91 season, when Aberdeen were beaten 2–0 to win the title for the third time. The day before the match he had a pain-killing injection to ensure he could train, couldn't walk on the morning of the match, still played with injections before and during the match and held the defence together until the damaged tendon ruptured altogether in the second half.

Any assessment of his worth to Rangers should take into account that he was the most-used player, with 59 competitive appearances plus another four friendlies during the 1992–93 season, when the club went unbeaten for 44 games and progressed to within one match of the European Cup final. Brown was a regular scorer for the club, famously including one in the New Year derby of 1992, and a rather vindictive six of his 14 goals came against Motherwell. He is now coaching at Ibrox.

Terry Butcher

Graeme Souness always honours Butcher by saying that if the inspirational captain had not suffered a broken leg in 1987–88, Rangers would have won their Nine-in-a-row two seasons earlier than they eventually did.

Butcher, even more than Chris Woods who preceded him, marked the revolutionary buying success of Souness when he arrived from Ipswich in August 1986 for £725,000.

An England captain in his time, Butcher became

Captain Courageous Terry Butcher in action for Rangers during a 1989 Old Firm encounter

the absolute cornerstone of the team on and off the pitch: an inspirational figure who seemed to adopt the club from the moment he arrived, having had initial doubts about the move north.

He lifted the championship in his first season, scoring the League-winning goal at Pittodrie and sharing in the reflected glory after nine years without a title at Ibrox.

But he missed almost half of the next term after breaking a leg against Aberdeen at Ibrox and Souness now claims that single injury was the difference between Rangers winning the title and finishing third.

Athletic, strong and tall, Butcher also had a good football brain which, twinned with Richard Gough's similar abilities, started to make Rangers close to impregnable at the back.

There were lows, however, including the court appearances he, Chris Woods, Graham Roberts and Frank McAvennie made following the wildly controversial Old Firm match on 17 October 1987.

But bad blood broke out between Souness and Butcher when Butcher allegedly "refused to play" in the 1990 League Cup Final, in which Rangers beat Celtic, leading to a dispute over whether the defender had been fit or not. It wasn't the proper way for such a mammoth contribution to come to an end, but Butcher was, literally, sent to Coventry.

Iain Durrant

Mention the name Iain Durrant to any Rangers supporter and his eyes should glaze over with happy memories; but instead, all that will be provoked are angry memories of 8 October 1988, when a crazy tackle from Neil Simpson shattered the midfielder's knee.

It is difficult to exaggerate how promising Durrant's career had already become, aged 21. Suffice it to say that he had already played 122 games for Rangers.

He looked as if he was going to have everything. McCoist and he, soulmates in the dog-eat-dog humour of the dressing room, were almost telepathic in their on-field runs and use of the ball while

---

Terry BUTCHER

Born: 28 December 1958, Singapore
Position: Defender
Height: 6ft 4in
Weight: 14st 7lb
Former clubs: Ipswich
League appearances: 127
League goals: 7

Iain Durrant scores his second goal of the 1995 win against Kilmarnock at Ibrox

Iain DURRANT

Born: 29 September 1966, Glasgow
Position: Midfield
Height: 5ft 8in
Weight: 9st 7lb
Former clubs: Glasgow United
League appearances: 192 (+50)
League goals: 26

Durrant's touch, finesse and finishing power made him look a safe bet as the fulcrum of Scotland's midfield for the next decade.

In reality, he didn't play again until 6 April 1991 – almost two and a half years later. 15,000 fans turned up for his first comeback game in the reserves and the club got their reward when his imagination and vision helped power the 44-game unbeaten run of 1992–93.

Against Rangers' most difficult Champions' League opponents that season, Marseilles, it was Durrant who led the charge by creating the equalizer for Mark Hateley at Ibrox and scoring for the draw in France.

What finer reward could Durrant have wished for than to loft the ball into the goalmouth when Rangers blew Celtic's lingering hopes of the 1996–97 League title out of the water?

Laudrup may just have got a touch, but any Rangers fan who saw the mercurial young Durrant flare into life in 1985, only to be almost snuffed out through injury, will forever give that crucial goal to "Durranty".

Ian Ferguson

Ian Ferguson is one of only three players, along with Ally McCoist and Richard Gough, who has been talented, durable and lucky enough to win a championship badge in each of Rangers historic Nine-in-a-Row titles.

Maybe it is Lady Luck's way of repaying Fergie for the grim determination he showed in 1987 when he repeatedly insisted he wanted to leave St Mirren and join Rangers although the £1 million deal took an interminable time to be agreed.

1988–89 was a vintage year for the midfielder, scoring in a 4–1 defeat of Celtic, an overhead goal in the League Cup final win against Aberdeen and a vicious

Ian FERGUSON

Born: 15 March, 1967, Glasgow
Position: Midfield
Height: 5ft 10in
Weight: 10st
Former Clubs: Clyde, St Mirren
League Appearances: 192 (+20)
League Goals: 23

free kick at Parkhead for Rangers' first victory there for nine years.

Unfortunately he missed a huge number of matches between 1990 and 1992 due to a combination of illness and injury, but returned to score the vital winner against CSKA Moscow during Rangers' spectacular 1992–93 European Champions' League run. The following season Ian held the midfield together, at a time when the club was in the grip of an injury crisis, playing more matches than anyone else.

Valued by his team-mates for his ability to cover so much ground, both in attack and defence, Fergie is never more dangerous than when counter-attacking. Now in his 31st year, he has earned the right to call himself a Rangers Nine-in-a-row veteran.

Paul Gascoigne

It has become immensely fashionable to disparage Bill Shankly's immortal allegation that football is more important than life or death, but those who do so fail to understand the footballing phenomenon that is Paul Gascoigne.

No one who watched his virtuoso hat-trick against Aberdeen to win Rangers their eighth title on the penultimate weekend of the 1996–97 season will forget the impact which one man, cutting through a team as if he is on radar, can have on them.

But after that outpouring of his genius Gascoigne gave an equally memorable performance, deep in the bowels of the majestic Ibrox Stadium, as he talked about what playing for Rangers meant to him.

Gascoigne has a plethora of personalities but that afternoon he was at one with himself and simply said, "I'd like to thank Walter (Smith) and Archie (Knox) for giving me back my life."

He had never lifted a major trophy in his entire

Ferguson's vintage season was 1988–89 when his overhead kick against Aberdeen helped win the Skol Cup

The hair may be a different colour, but Gazza is still running rings around the Celtic defence

senior career that day, and feared in the darkest days of his injuries that he never would.

Somehow, that season at least, Gazza the boy had become Gascoigne the man and his "fit" with Rangers seemed perfect. Football was his reason for living again.

Whether it was tormenting Celtic by scoring and making goals while winning each of his first two visits to Parkhead, "booking" referee Dougie Smith for dropping his yellow card, that brilliant solo goal against Steaua Bucharest in the Champions' League or the way in which he simply assumed command of the second half against Borussia Dortmund at Ibrox, Gascoigne was able to rub people's noses in his own superiority. That went down well with the blue legions, who don't exactly dislike a bit of justified arrogance.

After his second full season, Gascoigne had played in nine Old Firm matches, winning seven, never losing, scoring a couple and making a couple – genuinely the stuff of undying legend at Ibrox. Yet Smith went into print towards the end of the 1996–97 season to admit that Gascoigne's behaviour had often led him to question seriously whether he had been right to make the £4.3 million signing from Lazio.

Gascoigne blamelessly suffered an awful injury, which maimed his 1996–97 season, during the Ajax six-a-side tournament in January when Dutch keeper Fred Grimm tackled him ludicrously. At that stage he was beginning to play so cleverly again after being dogged by the traumas of his personal life and he just made it to fitness in time to help win Nine-in-a-row.

When news of his signature trickled out in April 1995 it was greeted with disbelief. Much of what he has since done on and off the pitch is equally incredible. But Paul Gascoigne remains, to all Rangers fans, unbelievable.

Paul GASCOIGNE

Born: 27 May 1967, Gateshead
Position: Midfield
Height: 5ft 9in
Weight: 11st 11lb
Former clubs: Newcastle United, Tottenham Hotspur, Lazio
League appearances: 50 (+4)
League goals: 27

Andy Goram

Around Ibrox, Andy Goram is always referred to as "The Goalie" as if there could only ever be one him.

Andy GORAM

Born: 13 April 1964, Bury
Position: Goalkeeper
Height: 5ft 11in
Weight: 12st 13lb
Former clubs: Oldham, Hibernian
League appearances: 159 (+1)
League Goals: 0

Just as Pele's Number 10 jersey at Santos was retired when the great man moved on, the player to keep goal for Rangers in future will be known by his own name, never as "The Goalie".

At times during his career with Rangers he has given dozens of genuinely world-class performances which epitomize his utter hatred of losing. He was Walter Smith's first signing as manager, in June 1991, and ranks only behind Laudrup as his most consistent one.

Central to the decision to choose Goram was the fact that Rangers had failed to score against him in five of their last eight matches against Hibs.

But offloading Chris Woods because of the three-foreigner rule was vital to the move.

Subsequent years make Smith's £200,000 net profit on the sale of Woods and purchase of Goram seem like divine intervention. Goram has a bullish determination not to be beaten in anything which, allied to his natural eye-to-ball coordination and close reflexes, makes him one of those 'keepers who doesn't just block strikers out – he breaks their hearts.

He was the rock upon which 1992–93's unbeaten run of 44 matches in all competitions was built. His great value to the team has been his ability to withstand absolutely withering pressure on his goal from major competitors such as Celtic and Aberdeen until one of his team-mates scores on the break and the game can then be closed up.

Ask any Celtic fan about the misery Rangers have inflicted on him over the last nine years and he will tell you that Goram's brilliant one-on-one ability is the most under-rated factor.

It is hardly news to say that Goram has a lust for life which has, occasionally, interfered with his enthusiasm for keeping the ball out of the net; but when the short sharp shock of the transfer list was applied, "The Goalie" fought back.

His tutor is goalkeeping coach Alan Hodgkinson, the bluff Englishman who also works with Peter Schmeichel. At Euro '96, when the English media in particular were proclaiming the Manchester United keeper to be the world's best, Hodgkinson, without fuss, told observers at Scotland's training session that he thought Goram the better of the two.

"The Goalie": Drinking in the atmosphere in the 1996 match against Celtic

Richard Gough

Along with greatness, God usually bestows upon sportsmen and women a complete lack of understanding of when the time has come to say goodbye. Richard Gough has not only been the on-field pilot steering Rangers to their place in football history, but knew when to call it a day.

> **Richard GOUGH**
> **Born:** 5 April 1962, Stockholm
> **Position:** Defender
> **Height:** 6ft
> **Weight:** 11st 12lb
> **Former clubs:** Dundee United, Tottenham Hotspur
> **League appearances:** 263
> **League goals:** 19

With 263 appearances throughout the nine-championship run – 77 games more than any other player – who could have blamed Gough for seeing out the remaining year of his contract and stretching out his fingertips for what already seems likely to be 10 in a row?

Certainly Walter Smith wanted him to stay, and Gough's performances were still of a high-enough calibre, even at the age of 34. An astute reading of his departure is that as an intelligent man, undoubtedly destined to be a coach, he saw that David Murray now wants Europe to be the absolute priority; and while holding off the Premier League at 35 is feasible, holding off Ronaldo, Alessandro Del Piero or Davor Sukor might not be.

So he chose to leave before he needed to be pushed, opting to play in the far lower-grade Major League Soccer franchise of Kansas City Wizards. Gough could actually have had a 17-year career at Ibrox, instead of winning the Championship and League Cup with Dundee United before captaining Spurs in the FA Cup Final and finally moving to Rangers in a £1.5 million deal.

He had a trial period with Rangers as early as 1980, when John Greig's managerial set-up allowed him to go to waste. Twice Souness tried to buy him from United before eventually succeeding in prising him away from White Hart Lane.

Gough was also rare in his articulate, honest appraisal of the game which he was always willing to share, thus becoming one of the most dignified of the club's employees, certainly in the modern era if not ever.

One sad blemish on that record is the clash of wills between him and Scotland coach Andy Roxburgh in 1993, which was allowed to fester and then become outright war – robbing Gough of the chance to reach his century of caps.

His farewell present to the club and its fans was his astonishing ability to play against Celtic at Parkhead in the vital game of 16 March 1997, when their 1–0 victory all but assured Rangers of their ninth title. He had missed the previous two games with injury, definitely wasn't fit to play the way he did and was then forced to miss the next three games as a consequence – but that is Richard Gough, Rangers' Nine-in-a-row captain.

Few in Rangers' long history can compare with Gough's professionalism and desire to win

Mark Hateley

For those Rangers fans in the Ibrox chorus who sing "We are Rangers, super Rangers, no one likes us, we don't care", Mark Hateley is a soul brother. When the England international arrived in the summer of 1990 his reception did nothing to earn Glasgow its title of European City of Culture.

Rangers' fans thought that their new signing from the Continent was cumbersome, slow to react and, worst of all, a threat to people's champion Ally McCoist. No one liked him but thankfully he didn't care.

History now proves Mark Wayne Hateley to have been one of Rangers' supreme players: a rigorous professional, a fearsome competitor and a relentless winner.

By the time he and his team-mates reached the Wagnerian climax of the Englishman's first season for the club Rangers had frittered away their lead, Aberdeen needed only a point for the title and Hateley had scored only three League goals since January.

Yet Hateley simply trampled on Aberdeen that day in May 1991, scoring twice and taking the game not by the scruff of the neck but by the throat. His headed goal from a cross by Mark Walters was a thing of aerodynamic beauty and he handed Rangers the only victory in their nine championships which, if it were taken away on its own, would have ended the run.

Hateley's name is also stamped on Rangers' proudest European hour in the last two decades: 4 November 1992. Defending a 2–1 lead at Elland Road in the Champions' League and denied inclusion in the England team by Graham Taylor, Hateley was regarded as a has-been in his own land – but he destroyed Leeds.

If any other testimony were needed to the legacy of Mark Hateley at Ibrox, it is provided by Walter Smith's efforts to replicate his play by signing, or attempting to sign, Duncan Ferguson, Jardel, Alen Boksic, Gianluca Vialli, Fabrizio Ravanelli and Oleg Salenko.

Mark HATELEY

Born: 7 November 1961, Wallasey
Position: Centre-forward.
Height: 6ft 3in
Weight: 13st
Former clubs: Portsmouth, Coventry City, AC Milan, Monaco
League appearances: 162 (+7)
League goals: 88

Mark Hateley celebrates the first of his two goals against Aberdeen that won the 1991 Championship

When a last-minute signing was needed on transfer deadline day 1997, with a vital Old Firm match at Parkhead to contest, it was the discarded genuine article, then at QPR, to whom Smith turned. Hateley – surprise, surprise – muscularly contributed to Brian Laudrup's winning goal.

Mark Hateley - without him there would be no Nine-in-a-row.

Maurice Johnston

Mo Johnston's signing for Rangers has been viewed as an epoch-making moment simply because he became the first Roman Catholic of the modern era to play for a club which had been staunchly Protestant for decades.

But that must be revised on two counts. Firstly, that he scored 31 times in two seasons – a good enough return – but secondly, and more importantly, that his arrival cleared the way for so many other splendid players to follow.

Now it is regarded as simply good footballing practice for Rangers to sign several Italian Serie

Maurice JOHNSTON

Born: 13 April 1963, Glasgow
Position: Striker
Height: 5ft 10in
Weight: 11st 10lb
Former clubs: Partick Thistle, Watford, Nantes (Fra)
League appearances: 75 (+1)
League goals: 31

Whyte in possession at Ibrox but thanks to the tenacity and goals of Mo Johnston, Rangers won

A players in a close season: before Graeme Souness and David Holmes sensibly broke with tradition it was impossible, because the players were Catholic.

Johnston formed good partnerships with first McCoist and then Hateley; but, if truth be told, it was not until he scored the winner against his ex-club Celtic in November of his first season that some of Rangers' more extreme fans were won over.

In the summer Celtic had actually paraded Johnston as their player once more but the contract was never signed, and Souness persuaded the striker to switch his allegiance.

Sadly, it was a time of security guards having to check underneath players' cars for bombs, after repeated threats against the team succeeded the mere burning of scarves and returning of season-tickets which showed the nonsensical nature of embedded bigotry.

It was far from his only controversy, and after a pre-season incident which saw him sent home from Italy and a deterioration in his relationship with club management he was sold to Everton for the same amount, £1.5 million, as he cost on his arrival from Nantes.

Brian Laudrup

Few players become the personal obsession of a true footballing genius like Johan Cruyff, but Laudrup has. Since joining Rangers, Laudrup's household has regularly received telephone calls from Barcelona with invitations, which Rangers' owner David Murray correctly identified as breaking all of football's rules, to come and play for Cruyff and earn a king's ransom.

> **Brian LAUDRUP**
>
> **Born:** 22 February 1969, Vienna
> **Position:** Striker
> **Height:** 6ft
> **Weight:** 13st
> **Former clubs:** Brondby (Swe), Bayer Uerdingen, Bayern Munich (Ger), Fiorentina, AC Milan, Fiorentina (Ita)
> **League apps:** 89.
> **League goals:** 28

However, so happy is Laudrup with the reverence in which the Ibrox crowd holds him, his relationship with the club's management and his family's contentment in their countryside home that the invitations have never been given house-room.

Then, as soon as Cruyff resurrected his football career in the spring of 1997 as the major adviser at Ajax, it was the Amsterdam club which came calling on Laudrup with the offer of a chance to burnish his glowing career at their European academy of excellence.

Murray's willingness to forsake a £4.5 million fee with the risk of no compensation for Laudrup's potential departure in summer 1998 also speaks for itself. So rare is the talent of taking the ball past innumerable opponents as if they are glued to the ground that in the last four decades Rangers have had only three such maestros – Jim Baxter, Davie Cooper and Laudrup.

But the Dane stands out for his ability to stand a match completely on its head, with or without the help of his team-mates. Ten months after signing for Rangers he was Scotland's Player of the Year and his dazzling play had been the jewel in the crown of Rangers' seventh straight title.

Another 12 months on and he had another League badge, but it was his divine performance in the 5–1 dissection of Hearts during the Scottish Cup Final at Hampden which was his *pièce de resistance* that season. No one who saw it will forget the inch-perfect passes played without his having looked to see where Gordon Durie, given his hat-trick on a plate, was positioned.

No one will forget seeing such intricate control used at such high speed, and Hearts will never forget the way he slaughtered them that day. By May 1997 Laudrup was once more Scotland's Player of the Year, and fittingly it was he who scored the goal which actually clinched that Nine-in-a-row title against Dundee United at Tannadice.

Defeats in Europe are the only things which mar his time in Scotland. Over three seasons, Laudrup delivered five trophies for the Ibrox crowd. And he has scored goal after goal by ghosting past players in that unique way which has always, and will always, automatically bring a football supporter to his feet with a gut-wrenching roar of approval.

Brian Laudrup: a footballer of world class whom everyone in Scotland has been privileged to be able to watch.

A superb performance by Laudrup at Hampden in 1996 won the cup for Rangers and destroyed Hearts

Stuart McCall: generating power wherever he goes and against whom ever he plays

Stuart McCall

A little giant for club and country, McCall is the player every team-mate loves to see in the starting eleven. Signed a matter of days after Trevor Steven departed for Marseilles, McCall fitted in instantly and has been part of the engine-room of the club ever since.

Born in England, he initially chose to play for the country of his birth rather than that of his father's but fortunately changed his mind and has been an influential and versatile player for Scotland since. McCall is skilful but that is often disregarded because of the massive impact his high energy playing style has. Although he has had more than his fair share of injuries, McCall is a relentless competitor whose ebullient nature off the pitch accurately reflects his dynamism on it.

McCall scored twice for his previous club, Everton, in the 19xx FA Cup final against Liverpool and also scored in the winning Scottish League Cup final of 1992 against Aberdeen. But it is his ability to play either as an attacking midfielder, a right-back or a deeply defensive midfielder, guarding the back four, which earns him the appreciation of those who coach him. His Yorkshire accent remains completely unaffected by years in the Ibrox dressing room but at Euro '96 there was barely a better performer for Scotland.

Stuart McCALL
Born: 10 June 1964, Leeds
Position: Midfield
Height: 5ft 8in
Weight: 11st 12lb
Former clubs: Bradford City, Everton
League appearances: 159 (+4)
League goals: 15

Ally McCoist

Rangers' all-time leading scorer, extrovert and crowd favourite, Ally McCoist actually needed three invitations to join Rangers before making the move in 1983.

Had he not done so, the club would have missed out on 36 goals and many of the trophies which McCoist's penchant for scoring in finals and against Celtic have brought them.

A Rangers fan since the age of six, when he won a strip in a newspaper competition, McCoist has not only fought off the willingness of Jock Wallace to sell him but, late in his career, opted not to accept lucrative offers from both Japanese and USA soccer franchises.

Twice winner of the European Golden Boot for his scoring achievements, it remains bizarre that McCoist was not popular on arrival, having twice said "No" to the club, and also missed out on umpteen more goals thanks to enduring long, unhappy spells on the bench when Graeme Souness was the manager.

He never did convert Souness; but the fans, back in 1983, were brought on their own

Ally McCOIST
Born: 24 September 1962, Bellshill
Position: Striker
Height: 5ft 10in
Weight: 12st
Former clubs: St Johnstone, Sunderland
League appearances: 353 (+50)
League goals: 246

Another final and another goal for Ally: this time against Hearts in the 1996 Coca-Cola Cup Final

road to Damascus when "Coisty" scored a hat trick in a 3–2 defeat of Celtic in the League Cup final.

Whether he has been properly understood as the goal phenomenon he truly is will not be known until after he retires and followers of the club start to examine what they have had.

Perhaps no goal epitomises what people think about McCoist more than his overhead kick against Hibs in the 1993 League Cup Final – barely fit again after a horrible broken leg, and only seconds after being introduced as a substitute.

But it is no fluke that he has scored almost 50 goals more than any other player during the Nine-in-a-row, nor that he is the club's second-highest scorer in Old Firm derbies.

Already an accomplished television personality, McCoist has been a distinguished Scottish international scoring 19 goals, including one of his career's best against Switzerland during Euro '96.

David Robertson

Robertson was simply the ideal athlete to play wing-back in the five-man defence, with the wing-backs pushing forward, which Walter Smith implemented in pre-season training for season 1995–96 and used to great effect domestically from that point on.

Signed in summer 1991 for a bargain £970,000, set at a transfer tribunal, when his contract at Aberdeen expired, Robertson won increasing admiration and favour from the Ibrox crowd as he proved to be

---

David ROBERTSON

Born: 17 September 1968, Aberdeen
Position: Defender
Height: 5ft 11in
Weight: 11st
Former clubs: Aberdeen
League appearances: 183 (+1)
League goals: 15

An intelligent footballer, Robertson linked superbly with Laudrup on the left

a fiery competitor as well as a lightning-fast defender.

Almost as soon as Brian Laudrup arrived he and Robertson formed a superb partnership on the left and it was a mystery to many why a minor dispute between Robertson and Scotland boss Craig Brown went unresolved, meaning that a player perfect for Scotland's almost-identical system was never called upon to grace the national side.

Trevor **Steven**

Trevor Steven has been a connoisseur's footballer at Ibrox, probably the most intelligent reader of a game there has been at the club in recent seasons. Proof of his genuine European calibre came in the astonishing £5.5 million which Marseilles paid for him in August 1991, but proof of David Murray's astounding business abilities came when Rangers purchased the player back for only £2.4 million one year later when the French club hit financial difficulties.

Like his England international team-mate Gary Stevens, Steven had been outstanding in the dominant Everton side of the mid-1980s.

But at Rangers, Steven's career has been cruelly blighted by injury.

Although he has never failed to look like sheer class any time he played in a Rangers jersey, his finest contribution probably came in season 1993–94 when the club was riven by injuries caused by the strain of their previous two campaigns. Steven not only produced the inventiveness upon which entertainment relies; he worked as hard if not harder than the foot-soldiers in the team.

One key moment came in the League Cup semi-final of 1990 when he dribbled from midfield and clipped the ball past Theo Snelders to eliminate Aberdeen and pay them back for the previous season's defeat in the final. Even when Steven was asked to play auxiliary right wing-back in his last couple of seasons at Ibrox, after horrendous spells out through injury, he still looked in a different class.

Trevor STEVEN
Born: 21 September 1963, Berwick-upon-Tweed
Position: Midfield
Height: 5ft 9in
Weight: 10st 12lb
Former clubs: Burnley, Everton, Rangers, Olympique Marseilles (Fra)
League appearances: 130 (+5)
League goals: 16

Trevor Steven contributed much but was dealt an unfair hand by the God of Injury

Gary Stevens

It was Gary Stevens who scored the first goal in Rangers' first title season of their 'Nine-in-a-Row' run.

Gary STEVENS
Born: 27 March 1963, Barrow
Position: Defender
Height: 5ft 11in
Weight: 12st 7lb
Former club: Everton
League appearances: 186 (+1)
League goals: 8

Gary Stevens' contribution to "Nine-in-a-row", and to Rangers, has somehow been completely underrated – perhaps because he is a full-back, perhaps because there have been so many glamour players when he was merely a superbly reliable professional. Whatever the truth of the matter, Stevens was bought for £1 million having been central to the cavalier Everton side which had won trophies galore in England and Europe under manager Howard Wilkinson.

His time at Ibrox revolves around statistics; he was, amazingly enough, Souness's 20th signing in two seasons, and scored the first goal of Rangers' "Nine-in-a-row", against Hamilton Accies, on 13 August 1988 – his debut. It is not just quality that managers pray for when they sign a player, but reliability, and Stevens provided that by consistently playing football at the back and asking too many questions of most teams with his athletic charges up the right touchline.

During his six years at Ibrox, before a £350,000 transfer to Tranmere Rovers in 1994, no one made more League appearances than Stevens, who missed only three games in his first four seasons. Even when "Nine-in-a-row" finally arrived, three years later, only Richard Gough had made more League appearances during that run than this consistent defender.

Mark Walters

Mark Walters was an early prototype for the unstoppable wide play of Brian Laudrup, but long before the Dane came on the scene it was Walters's special knack of tormenting Celtic which won the fans over.

Sadly, he found some of his work in Scotland more difficult and less enjoyable because his

Mark WALTERS
Born: 2 June 1964, Birmingham
Position: Forward
Height: 5ft 10in
Weight: 11st 11lb
Former clubs: Aston Villa
League appearances: 83 (+5)
League goals: 25

It wasn't much to look at, but the Walters' shuffle always confounded the opposition

arrival unearthed some despicable racism in the game, but Walters still stayed for a profitable four-year stretch.

In the 1988–89 season the winger scored four times against Celtic, including each of the 5–1 and 4–1 victories at Ibrox, and it was his wonderful shimmy and deep cross which set Mark Hateley up for his rampaging header in the title showdown with Aberdeen on the last day of 1990–91.

In fact Walters was not only a healthy provider for the Mo Johnston/Mark Hateley partnership: in particular, he also scored more than his fair share before being sold to Liverpool for £1.25 million in 1991 – bringing Rangers a profit of £700,000.

Ray **Wilkins**

A complete thoroughbred, Wilkins won the hearts and minds of the Ibrox faithful after arriving at Rangers from Paris St Germain in the autumn of 1987.

For his part, the England international thanked Graeme Souness for releasing him from the "very dark jail" in which he had found himself at PSG, and repaid the Rangers boss with performances of consummate class and professionalism.

But Wilkins is as intelligent off the park as he is on it, and the combined effect was like the icing on the cake as in 1988–89 Rangers won the first of what was to become their record-equalling row of championships.

In that season Rangers won 5–1 and 4–1 against Celtic, Wilkins producing an absolutely breathtaking volley during the first of those victories to score a wonderful goal.

Perhaps that in itself accounts for the thunderous farewell ovation which he received on finally leaving the club, after a home match against Dunfermline in November 1989.

Ray WILKINS

Born: 14 September 1956, Hillingdon, London

Position: Midfield

Height: 5ft 7in

Weight: 11st 2lb

Former clubs: Chelsea, Manchester United, AC Milan (Ita), Paris St Germain (Fra)

League appearances: 69 (+1)

League goals: 2

The classic Wilkins' volley against Celtic, and that unique London accent, will always remain special

Chapter 6
The Managers

One of the hallmarks of Rangers' glorious past has been a succession of dynamic and innovative managers. From Bill Struth to Jock Wallace to Walter Smith, all have contributed to the aura that envelops Ibrox and Rangers

William Wilton

It was in 1883 that the young William Wilton, who was to become Rangers' first-ever "manager", joined the 11-year-old football club. That an athletic young man should choose football (having picked his sport), was no surprise, for Scotland was in the grip of football fever; but it is not known why Wilton chose Rangers in particular – Queen's Park, the leading side in Glasgow at the time, were also the dominant club of the day, already having so many members (at least 130) that there were several teams.

Wilton was not a magical player: in fact he was ordinary, and was never to challenge seriously for a place in the top squad. He had a reputation for identifying talent, but Rangers are due the same compliment because, instead of being allowed to drift away, Wilton's administrative and organisational abilities were spotted quickly and applied to the reserve teams.

In 1890 the Scottish League was formed and Wilton became its treasurer. There were 64 clubs under its auspices, and Rangers tied with Dumbarton on 29 points for the first Scottish League championship.

Wilton was a leading figure in moving Rangers to its first real stadium, at Ibrox, extremely close to the current location, and 16 years after joining as a player had become match secretary, but his first season was trophy-less. However, that first-ever League was shared in 1890–91 and the Rangers Sports Trophy was won. The first major success was in 1894 when the club lifted the Scottish Cup, a crowd of 17,000 watching their 3–1 defeat of Celtic.

In 1897, as Rangers again moved ahead of the pack by becoming a limited company, Wilton became manager and celebrated with the Scottish Cup, the Glasgow Cup and the Glasgow League. His first outright league title was in 1898-99 when Rangers won all 18 matches. By 1914, before the First World War's worst effects, he was thinking ahead, and brought Bill Struth from Clyde as the first team's trainer following the death of Jimmy Wilson.

The Wilton Era

Scottish League Championships: 10
Scottish Cups: 4
Glasgow Cups: 12
Glasgow Charity Cup: 8

Wilton's work included coping with the onset of professionalism, paying wages, wading through the interminable disputes of the early years – pitch markings, crowd invasions, ineligible players – and then investing the club's resources in making signings. He took to it like a duck to water. Profits were made, Ibrox was built (and rebuilt after the 1902 disaster) and overseas tours began. The stadium became host to the annual Police Sports which brought in extra revenue and a heightened profile – around the world – whose equivalent is precisely what the money-men of today's game look for. Strip away the century which has passed since Wilton became manager, and many of the things he was undertaking remain basically the same as the club approaches the next century.

At a time when professional football was uncharted territory, Wilton's greatness lies in these aspects, rather than in trophies lifted. On 1 May 1920, his team won a 42-match championship, having only lost twice, by beating Morton 3–1 at Ibrox in front of 30,000 people. The following day he was with a friend on a yacht at Gourock, on the west coast of Scotland just south of Glasgow, when he went overboard in bad conditions and was drowned.

Bill Struth

Bill Struth was ideally placed to take over, having already proved his worth to the club for six years. But the impact Struth was to have on Rangers could hardly have been predicted at the time: for Struth, more than any other person, imbued Rangers Football Club with most if not all the characteristics which have made it great and are treasured by its fans. There can be no argument about that.

To the hundreds of thousands who followed the club during his 34 years in charge, it was of course the trophies, the star players and the victories over Celtic which were the be-all and end-all. But, again with the benefit of hindsight, Struth's true importance to the club is the way in which, like a strict father, he took the young buck and made it into a man before sending his offspring to Europe in 1956 to stand on its own two feet and face the best the Continent had to offer.

Whether or not William Struth would seem an odd character today is open to debate, but the anecdotes, history-books and incessant reminders of him mark Struth out as a strong-minded individual.

Players did not climb the stairs to the upper echelons, where the manager's stylish office remains today, unless they had his specific say-so. Within that room they would have found not only Struth but his budgie, which flew in at the window one day and stayed. Struth, in contrast to his sartorially pin-sharp managerial persona, also grew tomatoes in a greenhouse at the end of the away terracing – apparently everything about him was blue except his fingers, which were green. Oddest of all were the various leftover fragments of bone, cartilage and so on, collected from players during operations, which he kept in jars around his office.

The Struth Era

Scottish League Championships: 18
Scottish Cups: 10
Glasgow Cups: 19
League Cups: 2

Once a talented professional runner, he always bore the committed athlete's belief that first was everything and second was nothing. The players already knew all about him, and his beliefs, but he did not use his promotion to impose any footballing thinking on the team. He was more a part of Rangers, the football club, than of Rangers the football team: they were not the same thing.

But in his first season, when, as in most other years between 1920 and 1956 the team was picked by a player committee or the captain, Rangers lost only once in 42 matches and won the League title by 10 points, with a record total of 76.

Struth demanded that everyone associated with Rangers thought of themselves as "the best", comported themselves that way and proved it whenever possible. He meant it sartorially; in modes of transport; financially; in football terms; the stadium attitude – everything. In time it stuck, inside and outside the club, and in many senses still does so today.

Struth also took "the best" to Ibrox. At least as important as a trophy list, again, is the list of signings. Alan Morton, one of Scotland's best ever, was signed from Queen's Park. Dave Meiklejohn was the first lieutenant, captaining the team and at the pinnacle of the pyramid of players leading up to Struth himself. Bob McPhail and Jimmy Smith became the club's two highest scorers prior to McCoist, George Young, Sammy Cox and Torry Gillick, and – an interesting curio – he also signed two of the club's next three managers, Scot Symon and Willie Waddell. Made a director of the club in 1947, he handed power over to his protegé Symon in 1954. Two years later, aged 81, he died.

Scot Symon

Scot Symon differed from Rangers' previous two managers in that he inherited a club which had already evolved its character and, consequently, will be remembered for what he achieved in a footballing sense. That is not to denigrate the massive success of Struth or Wilton in terms of trophies and teams, merely to recognise that Rangers Football Club was already an institution – and one which craved more and more success.

Symon will forever be associated with the truly wonderful players who developed under his management. Although he was still not the ultra-tactical coach of the modern era, he was the most directly involved in team tactics and selection of any Rangers manager thus far. But his main strategy was simply to buy or rear as many terrific players as possible, particularly those who thought and played the way he wanted – Baxter, Henderson, Greig, McMillan, Brand, Forrest, Johnston, Jardine, McLean. Already successful as manager of East Fife and Preston, Symon won trophies remorselessly with Rangers, including two doubles and, in 1964, a treble. Indeed, in his first 12 years Rangers won the title six times, the Cup five times and the League Cup four times; yet, with hindsight, it was in Europe that Symon excelled.

The Symon Era

Scottish League Championships: 6
Scottish Cups: 5
Glasgow Cups: 3
League Cups: 4

Rangers, like all the Scottish clubs, were way behind the best when the European Cup commenced in 1956, and occasionally learned this to their cost. But it simply cannot pass unremarked that Symon took the club to two finals, a semi-final and two quarter-finals in Europe.

His achievements in Europe formed the benchmark for all subsequent managers, and it was Symon's great misfortune that Jock Stein's Celtic became the first British club to win the European Cup in 1969 when they defeated Inter Milan 2–1. The same month, Ranger lost 1-0 to Bayern Munich in the Cup-Winners' Cup Final, having lost 1–0 to Berwick Rangers in that Scottish Cup shock.

By November 1967, with the team unbeaten in the League, having defeated Celtic in front of 90,000, and on its way to the Fairs Cup quarter-final thanks to a terrific win over Cologne, Symon was called into Ibrox and dispassionately sacked. Such is football.

Davy White

Unfortunately for everyone at the club concerned, Davy White prove the folly of Rangers' ways. White had shown potential in his relatively short coaching career, but the massive pressure caused by Celtic's success, and managing a team which needed to be redesigned, were too much for White. Sometimes a man's sheer presence, past reputation or utter hardness can cause a stand-off with a club which is thinking of sacking him – White didn't bring these advantages to his situation. It is his misfortune that on the last day of the 1967–68 season Rangers lost 2–3 to Aberdeen, his team's only defeat but enough to cost them the championship, which went to Celtic by two points. White's only full season in charge brought a Fairs Cup semi-final – an achievement, but it was lost to Newcastle – while the Championship, League Cup section and Scottish Cup Final were all lost to Celtic, the latter by 4–0. Two years and 25 days after being appointed, White was sacked the morning after a thumping from Gornik Zabrze, 1–3 at Ibrox and 1–6 on aggregate. White was the only manager in Rangers' history not to win a major trophy.

The White Era

Scottish League Championships: 0
Scottish Cups: 0
Glasgow Cups: 0
League Cups: 0

Willie Waddell

Fortunately Rangers looked within their extended family and bought in Willie Waddell, who had won the League and reached three Cup Finals with Kilmarnock, using all the experience gained during his 18 years, between 1938 and 1956, as an exciting winger with Rangers. In contrast to his vast playing time with the club he was a manager for only 29 months. Not only was it a time of success but also of disaster; in 1971, 66 football supporters, who had gone to spend an afternoon watching a the New Year's Old Firm match, died in a stadium staircase crush at Ibrox, and a further 200 were injured. Waddell regarded that

The Waddell Era

Scottish League Championships: 0
Scottish Cups: 0
League Cups: 1
Cup-Winners Cup: 1

Waddell: the man behind the 1972 Cup-Winners' Cup

tragedy – and the imperative need to prevent it ever happening again – almost as his life's mission.

Waddell also showed a vision in footballing terms which was rare even then. He had the judgement and faith to introduce youth into his teams, with spectacular results, and the strength of character to hand over power immediately he judged it to be necessary.

Of course, the European Cup-Winners' Cup victory of 1972 in Barcelona will always be his high point, but Waddell also brought Rangers their first trophy in four-and-a-half years with the League Cup of 1970–71 when a six-foot-tall 16-year-old from Dundee, Derek Johnstone, headed the winner in a 1–0 defeat of Celtic. After the marvellous 3–2 win over Dinamo Moscow in Barcelona, Waddell showed his intelligence again by giving the reins over to his assistant, the first hands-on, track-suited football coach in Rangers' history – Jock Wallace.

Jock Wallace

It was the introduction of one of Scottish football's most colourful, anecdotal and successful characters. A former King's Own Scottish Borderer, Wallace had patrolled the streets of Northern Ireland during the Troubles and fought in the Malayan jungle. As goalkeeper/coach to the Berwick Rangers team which knocked Rangers out of the 1966–67 Scottish Cup Wallace had been marked out as worth watching, and Waddell took him from Hearts to be Number Two at Ibrox in 1970. Rangers had the right man. When he was only nine, Wallace had gone to watch Rangers play Hearts at Tynecastle. He later admitted that buying a blue rosette for a shilling had been too tempting so, having spent his bus fare on it, he had to walk the 14 miles to his home.

Of course he was a hard man – his pre-season training regime, based on the torture of Gullane Sands outside Edinburgh, was legendary – but it took someone with talent and nerve to succeed Waddell immediately after Rangers had won their first European trophy. For many Rangers fans, Wallace's teams won two of their favourite trophies in the club's history. The Centenary Scottish Cup Final was a roller-coaster of a game and wonderful entertainment, but Rangers won it with Tam Forsyth's famously awkward late goal – the first Scottish Cup win since 1966. Then, still more importantly, it was a Wallace team which halted Celtic's nine-championship run as they went for a 10th title in 1974–75. The domestic treble was won on two occasions – 1975–76 and 1977–78 – with judicious use of long-serving players such as Jardine, McLean, McDonald, McCloy and Greig. But even though there were important new names – Smith, Cooper, Forsyth, Russell – Wallace left

The Wallace Era

Scottish League Championships: 3
Scottish Cups: 3
Glasgow Cups: 1
League Cup: 2 (+2)

Jock Wallace proudly shows off his silverware collection

a team in need of renewal when he went to Leicester immediately after Rangers' 1978 Scottish Cup triumph. Not that he neglected the fact: indeed, he is thought to have quit precisely because of the difficulties encountered in purchasing the players he felt were needed. He returned for a much less successful term in 1983–86, when two League Cups were won, following time at Leicester and Motherwell. After Souness's arrival, Wallace worked and then lived in Spain but sadly died in July 1996, while Rangers were on a pre-season tour of Denmark – only one year before they finally won Nine-in-a-Row.

John Greig

John Greig was chosen as the man big enough to fill Wallace's shoes: a natural choice, given his monumental playing and captaincy success and considering how well promotion from within had worked with Struth, Symon, Waddell and Wallace.

For a completely new manager, Greig's first season was a rip-roaring success: both Cups, the best European run since victory in 1972 and the League lost only in a titanic meeting with Celtic in the third-to-last game.

Although Greig is an Edinburgh man, his name and personality are so associated with Rangers as to be inseparable – indeed, he is still there as a PR executive – and Utopia seemed to have been achieved.

But flaws soon began to appear in the team, which needed major modifications. Celtic, Aberdeen and Dundee United all began to flower at the same time, and Greig's ability to keep on reaching Cup Finals – and winning regularly – began not to be enough. He had to cope with nothing less than one of the greatest periods of transition in the club's history, including the end of a number of long careers, the stadium-building and declining crowds.

The Greig Era

Scottish League Championships: 0
Scottish Cups: 2
League Cups: 2
Glasgow Cups: 0

At any other club than Rangers, Greig's record of four trophies in five full seasons would satisfy any critic. But in October 1983 he had had enough of the incessant pressure brought by lack of a League title and handed over to his former manager, Jock Wallace. One of the greatest figures of Old Firm legend, Greig also played 44 times for Scotland.

Graeme Souness

The catalyst to the single biggest leap forward in Rangers history was David Holmes' visionary decision to appoint Graeme Souness as player-manager at Ibrox. In the general hysteria surrounding his appointment, the fact that this was a huge risk went unreported. Souness had no managerial experience, no background with Rangers or in Scottish football, Rangers had never had a player-manager before and the club was in dire need of immediate success. Which only serves to indicate what a thunderous impact Souness had, not only on Rangers but on Scottish football, and the debt which the club owes Holmes, its then-Chief Executive.

For Souness, there were no rules. Everything he did then looks so simple now, so obvious – but no one else had even dared to think as big as he did. Heysel's tragedy meant English international players had no European football with their clubs, so Souness tempted first Butcher, Woods and Roberts, then Francis, Wilkins and Hateley to Rangers.

Rangers immediately lifted their first title for nine

John Greig in his first day in the manager's office

Graeme Souness's expression says it all: the sweet, sweet smile of success

76 • The Managers

The Souness Era

Scottish League Championships: 3 (plus 32 of a fourth)
League Cups: 4
Scottish Cups: 0
Glasgow Cups: 1

years, Souness became a swaggering, successful icon – and the crowds flocked back. Souness signed a Roman Catholic, Mo Johnston, and won that gamble. Souness brought his personal friend David Murray, a man unknown in football, to the bargaining table, and Murray bought Rangers. Transfer records were consistently broken, Celtic were thrashed and all the ills which had festered and grown since 1978 were cured.

But in true Shakespearean style, Souness's spirited disregard for the rules could also prove to be a thorn in his side. He and his players now admit that he was hot-tempered, abrasive and quick to condemn those who got in his way. The media often found themselves barred, and Souness felt that even the SFA were persecuting him because of his high-profile success and by the time an invitation had arrived from Liverpool to replace Kenny Dalglish, he was not unhappy to leave his native Scotland.

As it turns out, Souness is owed a huge debt of gratitude by Rangers not only for his ambition, ability and achievement but, even more, for attracting to Rangers both David Murray – another talented visionary – and Walter Smith, his replacement, who has taken the club to historic levels.

Paul Gascoigne and Archie Knox embrace, as Walter Smith prepares to join them to celebrate the clinching of the 1995–96 Championship title

Walter Smith

Historians may well conclude that fate has been a fickle friend to Walter Smith, even though it has been under his leadership, as a born and bred Rangers fan, that his club has equalled Celtic's seemingly-impregnable record.

It would have been impossible to believe, while Jock Stein's teams were racking up that championship-winning record, or when the Celtic fans were mercilessly ribbing their counterparts over the years, that a Rangers manager would one day equal – and probably even beat – that old marker, yet still have an itch left to scratch.

There is a strong argument that Rangers' achievement has been all the greater given that they must play their most determined rivals four times every season; but in the intervening years, it has become more and more vital that Rangers regain their European pedigree.

Smith is now probably the second most dominant manager in Scottish football history, and his achievements are unquestionably remarkable. But the new, three-year contract he signed in May 1997 opens up a fresh era of challenges for him and his club.

The beguiling and appealing prospect for Smith is that if he succeeds, domestically and on the Continent, he could for the first time challenge Jock Stein's hitherto-irrefutable status as the most influential manager in Scottish footballing history.

His triumphs in the 1990s totally vindicate the decision to award him the manager's job vacated so dramatically by Graeme Souness in 1991, on the express orders of David Murray.

Even astute commentators on the Scottish scene had understimated two strengths which Smith possessed. The first, vitally, was the complete trust and respect of David Murray – the cornerstone of their symbiotic relationship.

Secondly, Smith has real pedigree, earned in the finest classrooms, despite the fact that Rangers is the only club he has ever managed. At Dundee United, he and Jim McLean not only won the League and League Cup but took United to the incredible heights of the European Cup semi-final which was only lost 3–2 to Roma after Rangers had taken an initial 2–0 lead at the Olympic Stadium. It is a feat he managed, in effect, during the 1992–93 season, when Rangers' match against Marseilles in France was pretty much the Champions' League semi-final. During his six years in sole control at Ibrox, Smith has displayed a range of important skills. Besides his obvious trophy record, Smith has a record of inspiring enormous loyalty among the most important players in his squad. Despite never having reached these heady heights as a player, Smith is hugely well-educated in European football, urbane and cosmopolitan. Foreign players who sign for him usually find a kindred spirit, and British players enjoy knowing exactly where they stand with the manager. This accounts, in part, for his ability to raise the team not just for vital Old Firm matches, which he wins with metronomic regularity, but also for the mundane League matches all over the country which win Rangers titles. Over the years Smith has maintained close ties with Italian football, particularly the Milan clubs and Juventus, and 1997–98 will see vast Italian influence from Marco Negri, Sergio Porrini, Lorenzo Amoruso and Rino Gattuso, while Gascoigne, Laudrup, Bjorklund and Jonas Thern have all played in Serie A. Making a huge impact in the first year of a new team was asking a lot, but it is the springboard for an all-out attack on the European Cup – and an even more elevated position in the long and distinguished history of Scottish football.

"Pick a trophy, any trophy": Walter Smith with his collection

---

The Smith Era

Scottish League Championships: 7
League Cups: 3
Scottish Cups: 3

Chapter 7
Rangers' Foreign Stars

With more money available at Rangers than ever before, It has been the club's trademark in recent seasons to invest heavily in overseas internationals.

Jorg Albertz

Tracked for a long time by Walter Smith, Albertz has many virtues but stands out as a rare breed these days because of his natural preference for playing on the left side and the unbelievable power of his left foot.

An extremely confident and outgoing character, the fans warmed to him rapidly and his nickname, "The Hammer", didn't take long to stick.

Signed for £4 million from Hamburg in the summer of 1996, Albertz was behind the Rangers squad on pre-season training and it was therefore all the more creditable that he filled the left wing-back role in place of the injured David Robertson for almost three months. Coming to a demanding new club and playing out of position while still chasing your full fitness is some task and Albertz did well – particularly for a smoker!

Although Rangers will be satisfied with Albertz's tactical contribution to his first season at Ibrox, the fans will simply love him for ever when they recall his free kick against Celtic in the New Year's game, which took off like a John Daly drive and fizzed past Stuart Kerr.

Jorg ALBERTZ
Born: 29 January 1971, Germany
Position: Midfield
Height: 6ft 2in
Weight: 13st 2lb
Former Clubs: Hamburg (Ger)
League Appearances: 32 (+10)
League Goals: 10

An unusual pose for "The Hammer" – with his right foot about to strike the ball

Certainly it was the club's most spectacular goal of the season; but over-attention to that masks the fact that the German played more games in all competitions than anyone else in 1996–97, and that he scored 12 more in a good debut season, including a superb seven in nine games during the vital championship run-in.

Erik Bo Andersen

Erik Bo is definitely on the other side of the coin from Brian Laudrup. The Danes could hardly be more different: Laudrup the metropolitan-born aristocrat, Andersen the shy, rural late-starter.

But they share two things, at least. Each has a gift and each did enough to make Walter Smith place faith in them. Laudrup had already set the heather on fire in Scotland for nearly two seasons when Andersen's prodigious scoring attracted Smith to invest £1.3 million in buying him from Aalborg, in Denmark's Super League.

Erik Bo could hardly wait to put pen to paper: the lure of playing for a club where one home gate could exceed the number of fans who watch Aalborg play at home in an entire season was enormous. But more than the trophies, more than the wages, more than the 50,000 crowds, the prospect of playing with the gifted Laudrup week in, week out was like winning the lottery for Andersen.

Already breaking through into the Danish national team, Andersen calculated that if he formed any kind of partnership with Laudrup it would help his cap chances.

Erik Bo ANDERSEN

Born: 14 November 1970, Denmark
Position: Striker
Height: 6ft 4in
Weight: 12st 4lb
Former Clubs: Aalborg
League Appearances: 13 (+11)
League Goals: 15

Erik Bo Andersen scores his first hat-trick for Rangers in the match against Partick Thistle in April 1996

The only problem has been, as Smith pointed out on several occasions while buying the striker and again immediately after he arrived in Glasgow, that Andersen came to full-time football much later than is normally the case nowadays and has rough edges – even though they do nothing to hide his absolutely extraordinary knack of scoring goals.

The rough edges, which will be smoothed out the longer he plays at this level, mean that his running style, first touch and ability to link with the team can look awkward in the extreme.

But there are days, particularly when his confidence is high, when it looks as if you could tie his laces together and he'd still score a hat-trick.

He had scored several times in the Champions' League with Aalborg, against the best opposition, before joining Rangers and has kept up the prolific goal-to-game ratio which made him Denmark's leading scorer in the season before his move.

Since his debut against Hibs, which was a rarity in that he didn't score, he has hit 15 goals in only 13 League starts – with another 11 appearances as substitute. Add to that his brace against Dunfermline in the League Cup semi-final of 1996–97, and Andersen's record bears comparison with anyone's.

In the mass celebrations which have surrounded Rangers over the past couple of seasons, and the attention paid to the more glamorous players, the value of Andersen's contribution has been overlooked by both the media and, to a lesser extent, the fans.

In his second match, against Falkirk, the League title was still up for grabs and Gerry Collins's team went all-out for a win. It was a double for Andersen which guaranteed the 3–2 victory, and the Dane followed that up with a hat-trick in a 5–0 thumping of Partick Thistle. Those six points set Rangers up for "Gazza's Day" when the Geordie's hat-trick sank Aberdeen and won the League.

But if he does nothing else for the club, Andersen has guaranteed the undying respect and gratitude of his manager and the Rangers fans with two very different matches – both against Celtic.

On 2 January 1997, Rangers were devastated by injury and illness and Erik Bo himself was suffering with the 'flu. When he was called on, with 14 minutes left, the score stood at 1–1, whereupon Andersen promptly hammered home two blitzkrieg goals to send Smith on THAT celebration run up and down the touchline. An absolutely vital win and central to "Nine-in-a-Row". Later that season, in the Scottish Cup quarter-final defeat at Parkhead, Andersen won football's equivalent of the Purple Heart for a sickening clash of heads with Alan Stubbs and was out for the rest of the season, but he had already contributed all that could have been expected from him – perhaps more. Erik Bo has already attracted plenty of attention from Continental clubs eager to tempt Rangers into selling him.

Joachim Bjorklund

Bjorklund arrived at Ibrox under Walter Smith with almost the perfect pedigree for Rangers, and has not failed to deliver. Not only does he have massive experience at international level – and in a team which reached the semi-finals of Euro '92 and USA '94 – but he has an equal amount of vital European experience, first with Swedish side Gothenborg and then in Serie A with Vicenza.

Joachim BJORKLUND

Born: 15 March 1971, Sweden
Position: Defender
Height: 5ft 11in
Weight: 12st 8lb
Former Clubs: Gothenborg, Vicenza
League Appearances: 29
League Goals: 0

Language has not been a problem, nor has integration with the dressing room, and he has adapted quickly to Scotland's climate and pitches. Add to that Bjorklund's impressive pace and marking abilities and it is easy to see why Rangers paid £1.7 million for the Swede in summer 1996. Naturally athletic, level-headed and someone who shuns the spotlight, Bjorklund adds balance in a squad full of "star" performers. Managers love players like him who can be relied upon, and Smith always insists he doesn't expect a a foreign import to reach his maximum level of performance in his first season. By that logic, Bjorklund has been a huge success already; and if there is more to come as he settles in and helps blood new signings such as Lorenzo Amoruso and Stale Stensaas, then that £1.7 million was a shrewd investment. After an indifferent Scottish Cup quarter-final against Celtic, his game was on a completely different level 10 days later in the crucial League victory at Parkhead. All this – and he's still only 26.

"Jockey" Bjorklund goes about his business quietly and effectively

Basile Boli

Really, the only reason Boli's season at Ibrox is often described as a let-down is because of the massive expectation and excitement which surrounded his signing – not because Boli was a flop.

Only Laudrup played more League games in a season when the seventh consecutive championship was lifted. But Boli had scored the winning goal for Marseilles in the European Cup Final against Milan in May 1993, after performing well against Rangers in the Champions' League, and had been a long-admired French international defender.

His arrival should have added an extra dimension to Rangers' game, but it was not a cup season and the early defeat against AEK Athens in Europe was a bitter pill to swallow. Boli reportedly criticised tactics and team-mates after the second leg, and although explanations smoothed the early difficulties (which can happen with any new player) his outspokenness tended to capture more headlines than his performance on the pitch.

But the worst mistake he made was failing, like Salenko, to recognise the massive *esprit de corps* which exists in the Ibrox dressing-room and shunning the chance to integrate properly. Having failed to do that, departure was inevitable and Monaco paid £2 million for him in the summer of 1995. Now playing in Japan's J League, Boli let himself down at Ibrox.

Basile BOLI

Born: 2 January 1967, Ivory Coast
Position: Defender
Height: 5ft 11in
Weight: 13st 2lb
Former Clubs: Marseille (Fra)
League Appearances: 28
League Goals: 2

Boli had the potential to become an Ibrox legend, but he let himself down during his spell at Rangers

Pieter Huistra

Pieter Huistra was another player who demonstrated that Ibrox likes wingers

It took the Dutch winger some time to find his feet in Scottish football, but the truth was that he had too much skill not to be a success. He was one of a succession of wingers invested in by the club in the last two decades – Cooper, Walters, Gordon, Huistra, Laudrup, even Mikhailitchenko at times – and the return was hours of fun for the fans as opposition defenders were tormented. But Huistra also had the knack of turning his skills into goals, and 22 is not a bad total considering the number of times he started a match on the bench. Moreover, there was a spell during 1994–95 when he and Laudrup starred on either wing, and Rangers were wonderful, old-fashioned entertainment. Like Laudrup, Huistra formed a good partnership with David Robertson, before leaving for Japan in January 1995.

Pieter HUISTRA

Born: 18 January 1967, Goenga, Holland
Position: Winger
Height: 5ft 11in
Weight: 11st 4lb
Former Clubs: Twente Enschede (Hol)
League Appearances: 87 (+39)
League Goals: 22

Oleg Kuznetsov

For any true football connoisseur, Kuznetsov's story has been one of the saddest during the Nine-in-a-Row. Already a well-documented international defender of European if not world class, he first played at Ibrox for Dinamo Kiev in the Champions' Cup, but stood out for an embarassing blunder. It was not his fault, but keeper Chanov threw the ball against him and the rebound allowed Mark Falco to score before McCoist added a second to eliminate the Russian champions. Later, in 1990, he stood out for a brilliant performance in a pre-season friendly at Ibrox and, with a bulging dossier in Graeme Souness's office, was signed in October 1990. He starred in his first game, against St Mirren, was injured in his second and didn't play again for almost a year.

The 28 subsequent appearances he made in the League merely confirmed that although he was not quite the same player after such a serious injury and absence, Kuznetsov was class. Fans will never forget his glorious drive in the 4–2 Old Firm win of 1 January 1994 – the only League goal he ever scored. Kuznetsov moved first to Maccabi Haifa, then back to Kiev, and has now quit the game.

Oleg KUZNETSOV

Born: Kiev, Russia
Position: Defender
Height: 6ft 2in
Weight: 12st 8lb
Former Clubs: Dynamo Kiev (Rus)
League Appearances: 29 (+5)
League Goals: 1

Brian LAUDRUP

Born: 22 February 1969, Vienna
Position: Striker
Height: 6ft
Weight: 13st
Former Clubs: Brondby (Den), Bayer Uerdingen (Ger), Bayern Munich (Ger), Fiorentina (Ita), A C Milan (Ita), Fiorentina
League Appearances: 89
League Goals: 28

Brian Laudrup

See "Nine-in-a-row" Stars (page 063)

Alexei Mikhailitchenko

Five championship medals, one Scottish Cup-winners' medal and one League Cup-winners' medal are a good reflection of how wonderful a player Alexei Mikhailitchenko was – but everyone who watched him still retains an impression that Rangers only ever saw about 85% of his potential realised.

He was what Italian and Spanish football calls a "fantasy player", capable of almost anything. One-on-one, he could dribble or sprint past defenders; his footballing brain and vision made him a terrific team player and meant that those around him could receive exquisite passes, while he could also beat the 'keeper from most angles and some distance.

First and foremost a ball player, it was no coincidence that Mikhailitchenko played in winning teams at Kiev, Sampdoria, Rangers and the Russian national side – he was a winner.

But he had a dreamy, lackadaisical air, and certainly wasn't one for the beloved Scottish traits of sweat, shouting, tattoos on the teeth and 90 minutes of frenzied running.

In probably the least significant match of his entire Ibrox career, the money-making testimonial for Scott Nisbet, he chose for some reason to put on an exhibition of ball skills which only served to underline that "Chenks" was a very, very special player indeed.

Alexei MIKHAILITCHENKO

Born: 30 March 1963, Kiev
Position: Midfield
Height: 6ft 2in
Weight: 13st 3lb
Former Clubs: Dinamo Kiev (Rus), Sampdoria (Ita)
League Appearances: 74 (+36)
League Goals: 20

Miko gets away from Dundee United's David Narey: Miko's pace and skill were a joy to behold and Rangers' players always held him in high esteem, although he was an enigma off the pitch

Petric rises above the Alania Vladikavkaz defence to head home during a Champions' League match

Gordan Petric

Gordan PETRIC

Born: 30 July 1969, Serbia
Position: Defender
Height: 6ft 2in
Weight: 13st 7lb
Former Clubs: Partizan Belgrade (Yug), Dundee United
League Appearances: 56 (+4)
League Goals: 3

Petric has proved a successful and likeable Ranger who won a certain popularity with the Ibrox faithful right from day one, having been snatched from under the noses of Celtic who were confident of signing the defender who had starred in a European extravaganza in which Ivan Golac's Partizan Belgrade put the Scottish side out 5–4.

At Dundee United, he truly caught the eye when the team managed by Golac came to Ibrox in December 1993 and won 3–0, and then in the Cup Final of May 1994.

Signed for £1.5 million in July 1995, Petric has been a regular and consistent performer, either in the centre of defence, where he still looks most comfortable, or further to the right.

Although he prefers to shun the media limelight, Petric has an engaging, dry humour and enjoys the Ibrox atmosphere to the full. Like so many of his teammates he is almost always outshone by the flamboyant, big-name players – Laudrup, Gascoigne, McCoist, Gough, Goram and Albertz.

So it is vital to remember the high point of his time with Rangers: his goal at Ibrox in the Champions' League qualifier against Alania Vladikavkaz. No one knew how easy the second leg would become and it had been a nervy first leg, which perhaps explains Petric stripping off to his vest and embarking on a wonderful lap of honour round the park, waving his shirt in the air, before being booked for his celebrations.

Oleg Salenko

Oleg SALENKO

Born: 1970, Russia
Position: Striker
Height: 6ft
Weight: 12st 9lb
Former Clubs: Dinamo Kiev (Rus), Logrones [Ed.?], Valencia (Spa)
League Appearances: 14 (+2)
League Goals: 7

Now that injury has forced the Russian international striker to give up the game, it is hard to say a bad word against him. But it is fair to describe him as a disappointment at Ibrox. Arriving from Valencia as a late-summer replacement for long-term signing target Florin Raducioiu, who chose to stay with Espanol, Salenko's outstanding statistic was that astonishing performance for his country in USA '94, when he scored five times against Cameroon – an individual World Cup record.

But it was when Dinamo Kiev, also starring Miko and Oleg Kuznetsov, beat Rangers 3–1 in a 1990–91 pre-season friendly that Salenko first impressed Walter Smith. Salenko had always had pedigree, whether playing in Russia or Spain: it was just that throughout his career, the Russian had displayed a startling ability to fall out with people. In dispute with coach Carlos Alberto Parreira at Valencia before he was bought by Rangers, falling out with the national selectors, being sent home from an Under-20 tournament while breaking through on the international scene – Salenko rarely concentrated on simply playing.

When he did, Salenko was an intelligent-enough footballer with a powerful shot and a decent scoring record. But, again, at Ibrox, he took his eye off the ball and bothered little about the integration which is so vital if a foreign player is to deliver all that he has been bought for. His two most significant goals came against Aberdeen – one for a home draw and the other in the League Cup semi-final, which nearly sparked a Rangers fightback. His attitude impressed neither club nor fans, and Salenko was swapped for Istanbulspor's Peter Van Vossen.

Peter Van Vossen

The Dutchman has yet to fully recover from the trauma inflicted on him by his miserable spell in Turkish football with Istanbulspor.

Van Vossen remains a mystery to most Rangers' fans but is totally committed to the club

Peter Van VOSSEN

Born: 21 April 1968, Holland
Position: Striker
Height: 6ft
Weight: 12st 12lb
Former Clubs: Ajax (Hol), Anderlecht (Bel), Istanbulspor (Tur)
League Appearances: 9 (+13)
League Goals: 5

A graduate of Ajax's academy of excellence, a regular international striker with Holland and a competitor in USA '94, everything went wrong for Van Vossen when he left the Amsterdam club and moved to Turkey.

Having been in the squad for Ajax's 1995 European Cup triumph over Milan, and therefore at the pinnacle of the game in Europe, the winger suddenly found himself playing for a club which was right at the bottom of the ladder.

Leo Beenhakker, the coach he signed for, was sacked; the 40,000-strong crowds Van Vossen was promised could hardly have fitted into Istanbulspor's 13,000-capacity stadium; the club were languishing, nowhere near a challenge for trophies. And to cap it all, the President of Turkey ordered the phone in Van Vossen's flat to be disconnected.

Naturally he seized the opportunity to join Rangers when they agreed a deal with Istanbulspor to swap misfit Salenko for the Dutchman.

It is also fair to say that Van Vossen's personal life has been a distraction to him in the last couple of years, and Rangers have typically allowed him great freedom to travel back and forward to Holland.

That investment immediately started to pay back on the pre-season tour of Denmark in 1996, when Van Vossen's enjoyment of football was clearly restored and he scored a hatful of goals – some showing glorious finishing ability.

The new form held: he started the domestic season looking entirely different from the sluggish footballer who staggered away from the Turkish nightmare, scoring five times in three games including an astounding 7–2 defeat of Russian champions Alania Vladikavkaz.

But as the title moved towards its superb climax, Van Vossen's goals dried up, although he finished with 10 for the season in all competitions. Now the challenge lies with him, after the devastating summer which Rangers have had in the transfer market. Great days lie ahead and Van Vossen needs to show he has the ambition to force himself into the reckoning once more.

Chapter 8
The Stars of the Future

Everyone hopes that Scotland's clubs will soon start to benefit from emerging national talent – until then Rangers will continue to compete for the cream of the footballing world.

One of the most pressing problems facing Scottish football is that a lack of investment and organization has, over a number of years, destroyed what was once a cascade of skilled young players. Even in the modern era, players like Davie Cooper, Ian Durrant, Derek Ferguson, Ally McCoist, and to a lesser extent Steven Pressley, Charlie Miller, and John Spencer have tended to disguise the fact that a real dearth of talent was looming in this country.

The advent of a vicious circle which starts with increased crowds and commercial revenue resulting from success, moves on with increased transfer investment and culminates in driving desire to keep on winning titles and other trophies has meant Rangers, naturally, relying more and more on imports of one kind or another.

Souness shocked Scottish football rigid, and built a superior squad to any other club, with his daring raids on England then Italy, Holland and France.

Walter Smith has maintained a commendable desire to buy Scots, even after the three foreigner rule began to lose impact, but now the type of signings

Jorg Albertz, former club Hamburg's youngest-ever captain, is already a German international

which were once made in Gordon Durie, Ian Ferguson, Andy Goram, Alec Clelland, John Brown, even Ally McCoist, come from around the world instead.

The quality of signing Rangers require to compete in the top levels of Europe either doesn't exist in the Scottish game or, like John Collins, stays unavailable for too long. England's market has basically become a thing of madness with the huge influx of cash from satellite television naturally forcing transfer prices and budgets up at the same, ludicrous, pace.

For Rangers to buy in England it would take an extremely unusual set of circumstances – particularly when even clubs like Coventry, Middlesbrough or Leicester are beginning to be able to pay outstanding wages too.

Success is demanded every week of every season at Ibrox and, although there are ongoing plans to re-orientate and improve youth development, the immediate raw product is insufficient to propel Rangers forward at the correct speed and so investment elsewhere in the world is required.

Not only are players like Vialli and Ronaldo being competed for, stars like Jonas Thern will increasingly be tempted by the quality of a contract at Rangers when they choose to take advantage of freedom of contract moves.

Quality in-contract players like Sergio Porrini, Jorg Albertz and Brian Laudrup will still be bought and Walter Smith has spent the last couple of seasons developing a much more widespread, sophisticated and reliable transfer information network.

Smith hopes that this will yield better and earlier information, particularly in the case of young, outstanding talents who can be captured before their fees become outrageous, nurtured at Ibrox before they must be thrown in at the top level, perform over lengthy contracts and then carry a good resale value.

Two perfect examples of this policy in action are Rino Gattuso and Sebastian Rozental. Each has yet to come near his full potential but each is held by good judges to be in the process of becoming an extremely high-quality international striker.

Gattuso was signed without a fee because Rangers were alert to a loophole in Italian football, (a move which was ratified by FIFA), and Rozental captured for much less than he will soon be worth. But the net result is that it will continue to take an absolutely outstanding, or very patient, Scottish youngster to break through into the Ibrox first-team squad and stay there on a regular enough basis to become indispensable.

This dearth of Scottish talent is being addressed, but slowly and in a disorganized manner – for example, Rangers recently identified two budding young talents for a full-time apprenticeship, only to find that they had been allowed to play so much youth football for a variety of different teams that they had stress injuries, aged 16, and had to be ordered to take a year out of the game.

Sergio Porrini is a former Juventus player who joined fellow Italian Lorenzo Amoruso at Ibrox in 1997

Most football fans are also aware that, for the moment, there seems to be no possibility of agreeing a formula for compensating clubs which rear youth talent, only to see those players free to walk away without compensation to the club at the end of a contract. This makes youth development risky and costly. It may prove to be only a phase, but for the near future the rising stars at Ibrox will tend to be the new signings from outside this country.

Sebastian **Rozental**

Rozental already stands out as Rangers' first-ever South American signing, but he has any number of other qualities which recommend him, not least his talent and scoring record.

The articulate, genteel young man from Santiago, who was raised in an English-speaking environment because he was lucky enough to be brought up in an affluent family, is a footballing prodigy in Chile. He made his international debut while still only 19 and his goalscoring prowess also took his former club, Universidad Catolica, into South America's Copa Libertadores.

But when Rangers made themselves known to Rozental, he immediately agreed to move to Glasgow and that fact betrays that this is a player who very much fits the new Ibrox template.

Young, with the beginnings of a good pedigree, Rozental should bloom while he is with Rangers leaving chairman David Murray in the enviable position of choosing, long before Rozental's contract expires, whether even more money will be invested in extending that deal or selling the striker on at a profit. While Scottish football still makes it difficult to attract well-established international stars aged 24 to 28, Rangers' ability to spot budding talent in new, less-exposed, markets will be vital.

Already a well-received favourite with the support after the enthusiasm he showed for Rangers in the couple of games at the end of 1996–97 before injury struck him, the development of this Chilean promises to be a fascinating story.

Rino **Gattuso**

Without wishing to be repetitive, Gattuso is also a shining example of Rangers' innovative approach to the transfer market from early in the 1996–97 season. His abilities had been brought to the attention of Walter Smith by a respected intermediary and Rangers' extensive contacts in Italy went to work in checking the young Gattuso out.

Although he had played a handful of games in Serie A, aged only 18, Gattuso still had not participated in the necessary number before he could be offered a professional contract. As such, the player was one of the rarest commodities in world football – an extremely talented and promising footballer who was an amateur, not tied to his club in any way other than by good faith.

It transpired, after investigations, that Gattuso had the technical skills, great strength and promise which made him a must for Rangers. Secretary and director Campbell Ogilvie did an exhaustive rule check and recommended to Smith that the player could be signed without a transfer fee.

The deal was done towards the end of season 1996–97 and although Perugia lodged an immediate complaint with FIFA the world governing body took only a few weeks to back Rangers and endorse Gattuso's move to Ibrox.

His early days as a Ranger were marked by Gazza taking him on an impromptu shopping expedition to the Italian centre and buying him a suit worth several hundred pounds – just to stop young Gattuso turning up in his tracksuits.

With the addition of Porrini, Negri and Amoruso, Gattuso had plenty of countrymen to make him feel at home in the new season and made impressive early contributions in the Nike Family Day, friendly matches, the League Cup and League.

Jonatan **Johansson**

Johansson is another young player in whom Rangers are willing to make a speculative investment, in the knowledge that waiting until such footballers are 23 or 24 and established means a transfer fee of between £5 million and £15 million depending on which country they are playing in.

Johansson is a young Finn who has already proved sufficiently good to make his debut in the national team and made a surprising career move by exchanging Finnish league football for FC Flora in Estonia during January 1997.

He actually made his debut for that club during the long Estonian training camp in Cyprus where the national team was preparing to play their World Cup qualifying match against Scotland and the domestic team was building up to its League kick-off.

Johansson, although still only 22 and developing as a left-sided attacking midfielder, was in demand thanks to the present sensitivity of the international scouting network.

He undertook a trial at Chelsea around Easter 1997, but the London club remained unsure long enough for Rangers to agree Johansson's presence during their pre-season build up and catch the promising talent for the next few seasons. Instead of having to buy at inflated prices every season or rely on the trickle of talent which Scotland is currently supplying, Rangers are catching young seedlings and hoping that they will flower at Ibrox rather than elsewhere.

Lorenzo Amoruso

Amoruso was a target for most of the premier clubs around Europe during season 1996–97 and it is to the credit of David Murray and Walter Smith that Rangers emerged at the head of the bunch.

A linchpin of the Fiorentina side which went all the way to the semi-final of the European Cup-Winners' Cup, Amoruso is a powerful stopper who gave Ronaldo one of his toughest matches of the season when the Italians played Barcelona.

Rangers cannily played on the fact that Fiorentina needed to repay a large chunk of the transfer fee invested in bringing Andrei Kanchelskis from Everton and moved in with a bid which the Florentine club could not refuse.

The real drama came, however, when Manchester United topped Rangers' offer on the day that Amoruso was due to sign but the Italian flat refused the opportunity to even speak to United and chose to complete his deal with Rangers which he felt, thanks to the work of Murray, was much more attractive to him.

An Achilles injury, picked up while still playing in Italy, plagued his early days at Ibrox but his potential is for Rangers to become far, far more frugal in conceding goals at the top level and his ability in the air will, inevitably, bring important goals from free kicks and corners.

Sergio Porrini

Porrini's career could hardly have commenced in more Boy's Own fashion for a young man from Milan. Playing in an open trial he was secretly spotted by an AC Milan scout who reported back to the club on the athletic defender, who was only 13 at the time.

Porrini was back home playing football on the street outside his family's home in a city apartment block when his mother came to the balcony and shouted down to the boy, in front of all his mates, that AC Milan were on the phone and wanted him to sign for them.

He prospered there until he and Arrigo Sacchi failed to see eye to eye, Porrini still calls the former Italian national coach "a little strange", and the defender went to Atalanta.

From there he became part of the Juventus side which conquered Italy and Europe under the imperious Marcello Lippi, taking part in the Champions' League campaign which paired Scotland and Italy's champions.

Porrini is firmest as a right-back or wing-back but has often moved to central defence. He has a good tactical brain and is a huge disciple of the extreme physical training which all Juventus players receive from Gianpietro Ventrone – something Rangers will undoubtedly benefit from.

Stale Stensaas

Staale Stensaas, with the possible exception of Thern, settled most quickly of the 1997 recruits

90 • The Stars of the Future

Stensaas is the chosen replacement for David Robertson because he is a natural athlete whose greatest abilities are his surging runs in the left-back position and the fact that he is an extremely consistent performer.

Were it not for Stig Bjornebye at Liverpool, Stensaas would be the automatic choice for Norway at left-back – particularly since the extraordinary exploits last season of Rosenborg, the club he left to join Rangers in the summer.

Stensaas was one of the pivotal players in Rosenborg's surge to the Champions' League quarter-final where he and his team-mates held reigning European champions Juventus to a 1–1 draw in Norway before succumbing 2–0 in Turin. If such competitive performances against Marcello Lippi's team seem desirable, what would Rangers' fans give for Rosenborg's victory in Italy against the once-indestructible AC Milan which put Arrigo Sacchi's team out of the competition?

His English is very strong, which will be an asset in

Despite this defeat against his former club, Gothenberg, Jonas Thern has already shown that he is a dominant, classy midfielder.

the critical early months, when settling into the dressing-room banter, communicating with his team-mates in training and learning to blend with new players in a new formation must be achieved in crucial game situations.

Even Stensaas would not claim to be one of Rangers' glamour signings in the company of Thern, Amoruso or Negri, but the club knows that progress in the Champions' League in the next few years depends on conceding far fewer goals than in recent seasons; and if the Norwegian can reproduce his hard-nosed, belligerent form of 1996–97 with Rosenborg then his value will be at least equal to theirs. He was signed with words of praise from Graeme Souness ringing in Walter Smith's ears as the deal was completed. Days before Stensaas joined Rangers, Souness was completing one of his last scouting missions for Southampton and called Stensaas one of the best players in his position in the whole of Europe.

Tony Vidmar

The first signing of Rangers' new era, having been captured on a freedom-of-contract signing from Dutch club NAC, Vidmar is an Australian international full-back who can play on either side of the central defence or in the middle of defence.

Competent and athletic, Vidmar may not be the most glamorous of the Rangers squad but has set an important precedent. Rangers will increasingly use the incredible wealth they are accumulating to pay wages, signing on fees and bonuses which make them massively competitive against anyone in the entire European market.

The Bosman development will increasingly lead to players moving at the end of contracts for free, even within Britain, which is currently not the case, and within contract, as footballers are given the same rights as other workers. Vidmar was the first to join Rangers on a free transfer, simply because his contract was about to end, and made history as a result.

Jonas Thern

The Swede is a superb midfielder who should be at the peak of his powers for the next couple of seasons. Aggressive, strong, tactically aware and with experience at the very highest level with Roma, Benfica, Gothenburg and Sweden behind him, Thern is the first of many "Bosman" signings which Rangers fans can expect to benefit from in the coming years.

Against Scotland at Ibrox in late 1996, Thern gave a typically commanding performance to tease Rangers fans with what they can look forward to, and then agreed a pre-contract with the club only a couple of months later. His mobility, sound football brain and sheer drive will make him the heartbeat of the team, hopefully allowing Gascoigne to be liberated from some of the duties which detract from the Englishman's ability to open teams up with a pass or a run in the real danger areas.

Importantly, for a club like Rangers, Thern is an articulate and dignified ambassador for football and someone who will help Walter Smith attract other top-quality internationals to Ibrox. It is worth noting that Thern rejected numerous opportunities to stay in Serie A and opted for Rangers.

Marco Negri

Another example of Rangers' updated transfer policy, Negri made a wonderful start to his Rangers career. Goals in the Nike Family Day match and then against Gotu in the Champions' Cup preliminary followed by a duo against Hearts in the first League match were enough to set tongues wagging about this Serie A striker with the very British physical presence.

Negri has been something of a late developer at the very top level but he caught the eyes of Rangers' scouting network by scoring more than 35 goals in two seasons with Perugia – while they came up from Serie B, and in the 1996–97 season in Serie A.

His name was largely unknown in Britain because of Perugia's unfashionable status, but he typifies the signings Rangers hope to make. His technical and tactical abilities are of a high level and although he had a superb goalscoring season at the highest level in 1996–97 Rangers were still able to purchase him for much less than the going rate at £3.75 million.

Compared to the range of prices the club was quoted for Kennet Andersson – between £5 million and £7 million – when the Swede is five years older, Negri could prove to have been a good buy based purely on goalscoring, and a superb one based on value for money and potential resale value in two or three seasons. Negri was also a colleague of Rino Gattuso while the two were at Perugia.

Chapter 9
The Old Firm Matches

No Rangers fan needs the tradition of the Old Firm match explained to them – it is part of your birthright, something which you will fight tooth and nail to get a ticket for, talk about for days before it happens and for weeks afterwards.

The simple matter of 22 players in Rangers and Celtic strips meeting to play each other every few months has become a spectacular, controversial, lucrative and sometimes even enjoyable phenomenon which seems to be gaining in attraction with each passing season.

It started last century with a very ramshackle definition of player registration when what was basically a League Select formed the Celtic team in the year of their foundation and they, and the Rangers team, repaired to a local church hall for tea and sandwiches after the match.

In the 109 years which have followed there have been thrashings, disasters, riots, great goals, great players and all the eclectic elements which make sport a passion for so many millions around the world.

Early encounters

The couple of thousand inquisitive souls who turned up for that first match in May 1888 would be shocked to find that you could fill a stadium of 100,000 and more for these games, that it is broadcast live and in highlight form around the world and that it is the defining game in each Scottish season.

Legends, myths, songs, bigotry, industries and a healthy bar trade have all sprung up around this fixture and Rangers' recent domination has only fuelled each meeting with extra relish – but history shows that there is little new under the sun.

As early as the 1909 season (see *Up for the Cup*) there was a riot which developed out of the replayed Scottish Cup Final. If what happened then was repeated today there would be a Government inquiry: fires were lit, mounted police charges were repelled by a stone-throwing mob, fire engine hoses were cut and there was a trail of damage from the south side of Glasgow into town. Hundreds were involved, but just one solitary rioter appeared in Govan Court on the Monday morning and he was fined £5.

There have always been, and always will be, complaints that the quality in Old Firm matches is variable because the tension is too high and because they play each other too often.

The modern fan would do well to remember that in the past it was much, much worse because of competitions like the Glasgow Cup, Glasgow Merchants' Charity Cup, Coronation Cup, Dryburgh Cup and others.

In the 1907–08 season, for example, Rangers faced Celtic on eight occasions without winning once, six times the year before and another eight times the following season.

The astonishing thing is that in the space of those three seasons, those Old Firm matches were watched by 845,000 fans – and that was before the two stadiums could hold six-figure crowds as they were to do later.

The dark side

Naturally there have been dark moments, like in 1931 when an accidental collision between the free-scoring Sam English and the athletic Celtic goalkeeper John Thomson cost Thomson his life. It was a moment which stunned the country and brought 30,000 mourners to his funeral.

In 1949, Rangers beat Celtic 2–0, 2–1 and 4–0 in the space of 26 days, but these were matches of an almost unparalleled level of national uproar as trouble on the terracing and on the pitch led to SFA inquiries, a boycott by opposition fans and a call from one journalist for Old Firm matches to be suspended. It was in these years and into the industrial 1950s when some of the ingrained ill-feeling emerged with fans siding in line with the Irish divide and it is, thankfully, an ongoing priority at Ibrox to try and move away from this anachronistic part of the historic rivalry.

Although the less savoury incidents have still added to the legend, they cannot for one instant conceal that fact that every so often the Old Firm match produces scintillating excitement.

In February 1957, for example, 55,000 fans saw an outstanding 4–4 draw in the Scottish Cup. Four goals inside nine minutes in the first half, four more in 11 minutes in the second half, two coming in the final breath of the match when Celtic had led 4–2, and end-to-end football throughout – a match to live in the memory.

Surprises and formalities

And the oldest expression in the book is that every Old Firm match defies the form-book. Although it is not true, it is the norm; and what better example could there be than 1957–58, when the result which no Rangers fan can utter without a shudder, 7–1, was followed in the next Old Firm match by a 1–0 win for Rangers! Where else could such a swing take place?

The early 1960s truly belonged to Rangers when

Willie Waddell scores a penalty during Rangers' three wins in 26 days against Celtic in 1949

the city of Glasgow met to play football and, under Scot Symon, Rangers won 4–0, drew 1–1, won 3–0, 3–0, 3–0, 2–1, 1–0 and 2–0 in a 13-month unbeaten run between January 1963 and March 1964.

Sadly, the awful tragedy of 2 January 1971 is something which is inseparable from the history of Old Firm matches. Sixty-six innocent football fans were killed in a stairway crush and the only thing which can, in retrospect, be said about it is that thankfully the lessons have not been forgotten and nor have the victims.

The Scottish Cup Final of 1973 will forever be legendary thanks to Tam Forsyth's inelegant winner in a 3–2 match which ended Rangers' seven lean years without the trophy, as will the bad-tempered day of 14 September 1974 when Parlane and Brogan were sent off and Rangers won 2–1 at Parkhead – their first win there since 1968.

The unbeaten season of 1974–75 when the League was won for the first time in 11 years, the first victory of the Premier League, Davie Cooper's absolutely magical ball juggling and goal in the 1979 Dryburgh Cup Final – for every dull draw there is another "Raging-Bull" classic around the corner.

Rangers' "thousand-day" unbeaten spell against Celtic which only ended in November 1976; the 1980 riot after Danny McGrain's deflected shot won the Cup Final when riot batons were drawn in Glasgow for the first time since the 1926 General Strike; 3–3 draws; 4–4 draws; McCoist hat-tricks; own-goals; red cards; players in court; more McCoist hat-tricks – and then nine-in-a-row.

Old Firm classics

RANGERS 5, CELTIC 1
27 August 1988

With hindsight it is as if this match was specifically organized in order to mark Rangers' intention of embarking on their record-equalling run. But at the time it was nothing less than the most spectacular Old Firm result in years.

Celtic were reigning champions, having won the double in their centenary year, and Rangers hadn't won a Glasgow derby for almost 20 months.

Souness had made it abundantly clear to each of his players that he regarded the previous season, when only the League Cup had been won, as a wounding failure – definitely not something to be repeated.

Rangers' squad had been carefully invested in during the summer with the two front-line players being a first-class striker, Kevin Drinkell, who ended the season as top scorer, and Gary Stevens who scored on his League debut and didn't miss a match in the championship until May 13 – the final day.

The League Cup and initial championship matches had gone by without a defeat but the only significant pre-season work out had been the 3–1 defeat of Bordeaux in which Butcher, Drinkell and McCoist scored while the 0–0 home draw with Hibs in the second League match had been a real let down.

During the previous season's four League matches against Celtic only one Rangers striker, McCoist, had scored and the drying-up of the goal flow against Hibs, after a prolific few weeks, seemed ominous.

The day of the game was initially perfect for football with almost 43,000 fans creating the usual cauldron of noise and passion and the pitch in dazzling condition.

Celtic started like favourites and champions. Peter Grant's shot whacked off a post and Frank McAvennie put Billy McNeill's side ahead.

But Souness had warmed his players up with a pre-match talk of awesome proportions and Ray Wilkins, in particular, was about to produce a match-winning display.

Rangers' midfield of Wilkins, Ian Ferguson and Ian Durrant smothered Celtic and the goals flowed from that domination.

McCoist scored when John Brown, making his Old Firm debut, had a shot blocked and then Ray Wilkins scored with one of the most stunning shots in recent Glasgow derby matches when he lashed the ball past Ian Andrews from outside the box.

But Andrews, who was to have a miserable season, looked much more at fault just after half-time when McCoist's very speculative back-header somehow drifted over him while he seemed to concentrate on

---

RANGERS 5 CELTIC 1 (ht 2–1)

Rangers: Woods; Stevens, Brown, Gough, Wilkins, Butcher, Drinkell, Ferguson, McCoist, Durrant, Walters

Celtic: Andrews; Morris, Rogan, Aitken, McCarthy, Grant, Stork, McStay, McAvennie, Walker, Burns

HT 2–1 FT 5–1

Rangers scorers: McCoist, Wilkins Drinkell (2), Walters

Attendance: 44,096

the close proximity of Kevin Drinkell.

At 3–1 up, Rangers were in embarrassingly easy control of the match. Walters, whose season against Celtic was to be as good as Andrews' was to be bad, weighted a fine cross for Drinkell to head Rangers 4–1 ahead. Then the winger was set up by Ally McCoist who nipped the ball away from Roy Aitken – Walters made the scoreline Rangers' best against Celtic for 29 years.

With only 63 minutes gone Rangers were so dominant that Souness could afford to make up his mind to come on, for Ian Durrant, and take part in some showy keep-ball which, although it probably helped keep the score down, certainly put the icing on the cake for the Ibrox legions.

RANGERS 4, CELTIC 1
Premier Division
3 January 1989

Some of the euphoria of the early season 5–1 had been deflated by subsequent defeat at Parkhead and two consecutive losses, against Dundee United and Hearts in the month of December. But single-goal wins against Hibs and Hamilton had at least stopped the rot and the New Year Old Firm match held the prospect of Rangers putting a seven-point gap between themselves and Billy McNeill's team.

For the second successive time at Ibrox, Celtic went in front almost immediately and in highly dramatic circumstances. Wilkins fouled McAvennie just outside the area and Morris, the Republic of Ireland international full back, curled the free kick past Nicky Walker.

But it was also to become the third successive Old Firm match in which the team that grabbed an early lead also went on to lose.

Celtic were missing Derek Whyte from the defence which had won at Parkhead and were also without Paul McStay. Gradually the same thing happened as in the first Ibrox match of the season – Rangers' midfield began to dominate and allow Drinkell and Walters to cause havoc.

The turning point, which removed any Celtic threat, came when McAvennie broke his arm in an early challenge with Butcher. Despite persevering, McAvennie had to leave the pitch – but only after Rangers had equalized. Wilkins flighted a free kick, Ferguson knocked it on and Butcher totally outjumped Lex Baillie to head the equalizer. It was adequate compensation for the own-goal and awful performance which Butcher had given to Celtic in the previous 3–1 defeat.

Then Anton Rogan had one of his customary rushes of blood to the head and pulled Drinkell down in the box when no real danger was threatening. Walters gleefully put Rangers ahead from the spot and fans were already chanting for five.

Just on half-time, Ian Ferguson's shot took a wild deflection to leave Pat Bonner no chance whatsoever and, suddenly, Rangers were 3–1 on top and looking to inflict a hammering.

Somehow, the match regained equilibrium as Celtic battled hard to hang on to Rangers' coat tails.

But without McAvennie, Celtic never looked like troubling Walker again and, midway through the half, Ferguson slipped a cutthroat pass beyond the defence for Walters to run in on goal and score the fourth. Cue even more chanting of "We want five" and a famous Rangers victory.

Ferguson, out of picture, makes it Rangers 3, Celtic 1 in January 1989

> **RANGERS 4**
> **CELTIC 1 (ht 3–1)**
>
> **Rangers:**
> Walker; Stevens, Munro, Gough, Wilkins, Butcher, Drinkell, I Ferguson, D Ferguson, Brown, Walters. Subs N Cooper, McCall
>
> **Celtic:**
> Bonner; Morris, Rogan, Aitken, McCarthy, Baillie, Stark, Grant, McAvennie, McGhee, Burns. Subs Walker, Archdeacon
> HT 3–1 FT 4–1
>
> **Rangers scorers:**
> Gough, Walters, Ferguson, Walters.
>
> **Celtic:** Morris
> **Attendance:** 42,515

RANGERS 1, CELTIC 0
Premier Division
4 November 1989

Of course it was always going to happen that, eventually, Mo Johnston would score a goal against his old team – it was, after all, what he had been bought for, amidst such animosity.

Mo Johnston celebrates his game-winning goal for Rangers against his old club on 4 November 1989

But even those who know the irony which football enjoys throwing up could not have predicted that Johnston would score the winning goal with only minutes left on his Ibrox Old Firm debut.

Having been paraded in a Celtic strip that summer and taken by everyone, bar Graeme Souness, to have signed for the club, Johnston's arrival at Ibrox could not have been more sensational.

Die-hard Rangers fans protested, to the extent of burning season tickets, and there was an incredibly hostile environment in Glasgow for the Scottish international striker.

In the early-season 1–1 draw Johnston suffered a massively hostile reception at Parkhead and was tormented by both sets of fans for missing two relatively straightforward opportunities.

At the time there were still those who simply did not believe that Johnston had the heart to damage his old club – an assumption which completely ignored the fact that this was a professional footballer whose game and outlook on life had both been improved during his time in France playing for Nantes.

It is to Johnston's credit that he ignored the threats to his life made by extremists and finished the season with 17 goals.

Approaching the second Old Firm derby of the season, Rangers were fortunate even to be in third place – accounted for by their poor start.

In the first eight games there had only been two wins, three defeats and three draws but each of the wins had been single-goal victories courtesy of Johnston. Each had been against important opponents, Hearts and Aberdeen, and Johnston had then been part of a three-game winning streak, scoring on each of those occasions too.

Perhaps it was inevitable that the goal in this big game should fall to him, but the match was poor and with 88 minutes gone a draw seemed much more likely than glory for MoJo.

Celtic had hit the post, through Coyne, but Rangers had been more dominant in midfield and if there was an outstanding player it was Mark Walters who relished turning it on against Celtic so much.

But the cross, with two minutes left, came from Gary Stevens and Chris

---

**RANGERS 1
CELTIC 0 (ht 0 – 0)**

Rangers:
Woods; Stevens, Munro, Brown, Wilkins, Butcher, Steven, Ferguson, McCoist, Johnston, Walters. Subs: Dodds Nisbet

Celtic:
Bonner; Morris, Burns, Aitken, Elliot, Whyte, Galloway, McStay, Dziekanowski, Coyne, Miller. Subs: Grant, Walker

HT 0–0 FT 1–0

Scorer: Johnston
Attendance: 41,598

Morris's swipe at the ball left Johnston in space about 15 yards out. He controlled with one touch and clipped it past Bonner with the next before being booked for the length of time he spent celebrating.

Any Rangers fan who wasn't won over by Johnston that day simply would never be, as he propelled the club to the top of the League, leapfrogging both Celtic and Aberdeen.

RANGERS 2, CELTIC 1
League Cup Final
28 October 1990

> **RANGERS 2**
> **CELTIC 1 (ht 0–0)**
>
> **Rangers:**
> Woods; Stevens, Munro, Gough, Spackman, Brown, Steven, Hurlock, McCoist, Hateley, Walters.
> Subs: Ferguson, Huistra
>
> **Celtic:**
> Bonner; Grant, Wdowczyk, Fulton, Elliot, Rogan, Miller, McStay, Dziekanowski, Creaney, Collins.
> Subs: Morris, Hewitt
>
> HT 0–0 FT 1–1 (AET 2–1)
>
> **Rangers scorers:**
> Walters, Gough
> **Celtic scorer:** Elliot
>
> **Attendance:** 62,817

The build-up to an Old Firm Cup Final has rarely been as dramatic for Rangers as, four days earlier, the team crashed 3–0 to Red Star Belgrade and, behind closed doors, Souness and Butcher fell out irrevocably.

Rangers had beaten Aberdeen 1–0 in the semi-final thanks to some ball-juggling skills and a neat finish from Trevor Steven, but the previous League match had been a 0–0 draw with St Johnstone and Red Star had as good as ended the European Cup campaign.

The last three League Cup finals had been classic battles with Aberdeen but the only defeat had been the previous year, so Souness was particularly keen to turn Celtic over in this final.

Butcher had been struggling for form and fitness after a summertime operation and, although each man's version of events differs, the captain did not play against Celtic despite Souness requesting him to do so.

Richard Gough inherited the captaincy for the first time in a cup final and marshalled the same defence which had been so badly exposed in Belgrade.

The game was thrilling, with all the skill and incident it is fair to expect from such a fear-filled occasion as a Glasgow derby played for silverware.

For Celtic, who always appeared to be clutching the game with their fingernails, Paul McStay and Paul

The quality most needed in a Glasgow derby – grim determination not to lose

Elliot were both outstanding performers, but Rangers again gave the better team performance with Walters tormenting Anton Rogan and Richard Gough giving a inspirational example – right up until the last moment.

Celtic's lead came from astonishing improvization by Elliot who dived instinctively to head home a low Darius Wdowczyk shot.

It hit the net with only 38 minutes left and the game nicely even, McCoist and Creaney each having missed good chances, but Rangers never looked beaten.

A probing ball from Gough, with 24 minutes left, was met by Hateley whose striking partner, McCoist, set up Walters for a goal-scoring drive.

The turning point in extra time probably came when the mesmeric Pole Darius Dziekanowski was set up to score but plonked the ball into the hands of Woods.

A few minutes later Bonner and Morris self-destructed when they both went for Gary Stevens' free kick, colliding for the ball to land near Gough. The new captain swivelled like a striker and hooked home the winning goal – to scenes of massive Hampden jubilation.

Mark Hateley causing trouble for the green and white defence in 1990

RANGERS 1, CELTIC 0
Premier Division
31 March 1992

Other matches during the nine championship-winning seasons better sum up the footballing values of Souness or Walter Smith but not one better sums up the essential spirit which breathes through the squad.

Beaten badly, 10 days previously at Ibrox by a Celtic side which encountered a surprising lack of resistance, Rangers didn't feel like underdogs in the build up to this semi-final but were widely considered to be just that.

Hampden was a seething mass of 45,000 fans being soaked by the absolute torrent of rain which poured down all night and the atmosphere was stoked with only minutes gone.

David Robertson had been teased all week in training after a tough match against his old Aberdeen team-mate Joe Miller in the Ibrox defeat. Six minutes into this meeting, Robertson used his body to block one of Miller's runs – it was his first challenge of any note but Referee Waddell immediately sent him off.

Momentarily there was mayhem as protests stormed in, but the odds remained stacked against the 10-man Rangers side who reverted to a simple formation with McCoist playing as the solitary striker – not a style which has best suited him over his career.

Set against the loss of Hateley, who had scored in the quarter-final and would do so again in the final, was the fact that Gough replaced Nisbet from the team which had been beaten at Ibrox.

Huistra was in for Mikhailichenko and the importance of adding two fighters like Durrant and Dale Gordon was to become apparent.

Although Celtic hardly scorned their man advantage they were far from dominant, and as the match became a test of who wanted victory more and who had the sheer strength of will to deal with the foul conditions, Rangers increasingly looked as if they had more self-belief.

This Scottish Cup campaign was Walter Smith's first in charge and the players were aware that the competition was held in greater esteem than in Souness's time. Comments in the press after the League defeat had been used to goad the squad in its approach to the semi and all of these factors conspired to bring one of the great performances under Smith.

Just before half-0time, with Celtic clearly frustrated at their inability to take advantage of the left-back's sending off, O'Neil took possession in deep midfield.

McCall nipped the ball away from him thanks to aggressive foraging and quick feet. With McCoist peeling away, McCall fed the striker who pushed on and finished by shooting earlier than Gordon Marshall expected. The goal was his 30th of the season and fuelled Rangers' belief that nothing could beat them that night.

After the break, Celtic hit the woodwork three times, with McStay's shot the most threatening of the lot, but Brown at left-back and Spackman as auxiliary centre-half next to Gough never looked as if they were filling in.

Old Firm classics

**RANGERS 1
CELTIC 0 (ht 0–0)**

Rangers:
Goram; Stevens, Robertson, Gough, Spackman, Brown, Gordon, McCall, McCoist, Durrant, Huistra

Celtic:
Marshall; Morris, Boyd, O'Neil, Mowbray, Whyte, Miller, McStay, Creaney, Nicholas, Collins

HT 1–0 FT 1–0

Scorer: McCoist
Attendance: 45,191

Instead Rangers almost looked as if they were toying with Celtic at times, so good were the passing patterns – even a penalty shout at the end when Collins went down was ignored and a famous Hampden match was won.

The statistics were overwhelming – the three previous Scottish Cup campaigns had been ended by Celtic, it was Rangers' first Scottish Cup final for three years and the Cup hadn't been won for 11 long years. It was this year, and the Celtic victory also set Rangers up for five wins and a draw in their last six League games – enough for the League and Cup double.

CELTIC 1, RANGERS 3
Premier Division
1 January 1992

Perhaps the title wasn't quite won, officially, with this result but the 10-point gap it opened up was the same one which the table showed at the end of the season on 2 May and the victory was spirit-sapping for Celtic.

Moreover this was a cracking good advert for the Old Firm match with each side genuinely on top for equivalent spells, two very good goals and plenty of controversy.

The nasty afternoon hadn't discouraged over 51,000 people from turning up at Parkhead and they saw Rangers play with all the purpose and assurance of a team buoyed by six successive wins before this Glasgow head-to-head.

Dale Gordon put McCoist away but he tried for show as well as effect and his chip landed just wide of the post when a more direct finish would have paid dividends. Hateley, more unusually still, missed a terrific headed opportunity, from a McCoist cross, by heading over the bar.

Celtic weathered that and then started to play a little through McStay (who was probably the man of the match) and Collins before Rangers gobbled up a mistake for the opening goal.

Grant was caught on the ball by Spackman and the Englishman beat two more Celts before finding Gordon on the right wing.

Hateley's touch on Gordon's cross brought the ball perfectly to McCoist who bumped it neatly past Marshall.

Big Tony Mowbray knocked in a powerful diving header in the 50th minute to equalize and then controversy erupted.

Brown had entered from the subs' bench and almost immediately sent McCoist in on goal. Marshall saved well at his feet but as the two stood up to chase the ball McCoist seemed to be impeded and the penalty was given.

Hateley scored his first-ever competitive penalty for Rangers and it was 2–1.

McStay had been driving Celtic on and it was not until he was sent away three times to sort a head-cut, which was seeping blood after a clash, that his and his team's rhythm dissipated.

Extra pizzazz was added to a hugely entertaining Rangers victory when John Brown picked the ball up just inside Celtic's half. Defenders stood off, Brown galloped on and struck a low hard shot off Marshall's post and into the net from 20 yards. His celebrations were carried on behind the goal and in front of ecstatic fans in blue and white who loved seeing one of their own apply the *coup de grace*.

**CELTIC 1
RANGERS 3 (ht 0–1)**

Rangers:
Goram, Stevens, Robertson, Gough, Spackman, Kuznetzov, Gordon, McCall, McCoist, Hateley, Mikhailichenko.
Subs: Brown, Huistra

Celtic:
Marshall, Morris, McNally, Grant, Mowbray, Whyte, Galloway, McStay, Coyne, Cascarino, Collins.
Subs: Creaney, Fulton

HT 0–1 FT 3–1

Rangers scorers:
McCoist, Hateley, Brown
Celtic scorers:
Mowbray

Attendance:
51,789

CELTIC 0 RANGERS 1
Premier Division
14 November 1996

This evening match was one of the most compelling, extraordinary and incident-packed Old Firm meetings for many, many years.

Perhaps strange incidents are forced out into the open when the correct amount of pressure is applied

Gough, one of the goalscorers, gets stuck in during Rangers' 3–1 victory, 14 November, 1996. It was one of most extraordinary Old Firm matches ever

to them, which is just about the only way to explain what happened.

Celtic had pegged Rangers back since the first derby of the season when Gascoigne and Gough had given Walter Smith's team a quite comprehensive win on the day and the lead in the championship.

In fact, Celtic were top of the table on goal difference and were welcoming Rangers to Parkhead with their first chance for many months to force their opponents on to the back foot.

Instead, Rangers once again suckered Celtic into exposing themselves, albeit only slightly, but Rangers were able to take quick advantage and struck with venomous pace.

Brian O'Neil somehow found himself leaden-footed as soon as he received the ball and fell over while trying to deal with possession.

Laudrup seized on the mistake, pushed towards Stubbs who was on the wrong foot and then lashed the ball across Kerr for a goal.

Smith had chosen to play the Dane as a solo striker, with McCoist on the bench, yet Celtic still had not learned how to deal with this proposition.

Had it not been for Kerr, Laudrup would have added another before things truly went mad.

The infamous Parkhead fox scurried around the pitch, in front of what must have been an incredulous Sky Television audience throughout Britain and Europe, obviously scared out of his den by the furious noise.

Then Gascoigne sloppily missed a penalty which would have wrapped up the victory before Van Hoijdonk did exactly the same thing at the other end.

As Celtic raggedly tried to throw numbers forward, Rangers ran through on goal time after time – always failing to convert their numerous chances for one reason or another.

Then came the moment which confirmed that this was the strangest of all nights.

Albertz broke away in complete isolation from any defender, powered into the box and chose to lay the ball off to Van Vossen once goalkeeper Stuart Kerr was fully committed.

The Dutchman was only a few yards out, with no challengers near him, yet managed to side-foot the ball up and over a completely gaping and inviting net.

It was an astonishing moment in a match which could have ended with several goals but instead ended with something of Celtic's spirit broken, with Rangers that litte bit closer to nine in a row and with Laudrup still a class above everyone else – even in the midst of a madhouse.

**CELTIC 0
RANGERS 1 (ht 0–1)**

Rangers:
Goram; Clelland, Robertson, Gough, Moore, Bjorklund, Petric, Gascoigne, McInnes Albertz, Laudrup.
Subs: McCoist, Van Vossen.

Celtic:
Kerr; Boyd, O'Neil, McNamara, Stubbs, Canio, Wighurst, Grant, Van Hooijdonk, Thom, Donnelly.
Subs: McKinlay, Cadete

HT 0–1 FT 0–1

Rangers scorer: Laudrup
Attendance: 50,041

CELTIC 0, RANGERS 1
Premier Division
16 March 1997

Just like the Scottish Cup semi-final win of 1992 this was a match which told its own story about attitude, strength of character and will to win.

Ten days previously Rangers had failed to sparkle in a 2–0 defeat at Parkhead which bundled them out of the Cup and prompted many to predict that a combination of form and injury problems was going to hand this vital match to Celtic too.

A home defeat to Dundee United had followed that loss, Goram was missing through injury as were David Robertson, Gazza and Erik Bo Andersen who had fractured his skull in the Celtic match.

Richard Gough was barely fit, Andy Dibble was out of Man City's first team before arriving on loan to make his Old Firm debut and Mark Hateley was rescued from QPR on a short-term deal aimed at combating Rangers' lack of threat up-front.

The game itself was understandably low on real quality, riddled with controversial incident and won by a goal of improvization.

Dibble proved to have a steady nerve and Hateley managed to disrupt Celtic's defence for the single goal which won the match.

Durrant chased what looked like an unproductive piece of possession and flicked the ball over Stuart Kerr.

In the goalmouth melee it looked like a 50/50 chance between Laudrup and the Celtic defender Mackay but the Dane showed greater co-ordination and foot speed to ensure the ball went in.

Although Hateley was subsequently sent off for his part in a multi-player barging match, the Celtic challenge faded and the whole affair ended with numerous bickering matches, even as the teams went down the tunnel at full-time. But this backs-to-the-wall display, particularly by Gough and Durrant, was the one which truly meant Rangers could all but touch their ninth consecutive title.

CELTIC 0 RANGERS 1 (ht 0–1)

Rangers: Dibble; Clelland, Albertz, Gough, McLaren, Bjorklund, Moore, Ferguson, Durrant, Hateley, Laudrup. Subs McCoist, Miller

Celtic: Kerr; Annoni, McLanley, McNamara, Mackay, Grant, Di Canio, McKay, Stubbs, O'Donnell, Cadete. Subs Hannah, Donnelly

HT 0–1 FT 0–1

Scorer: Laudrup

Attendance: 49,929

Hateley's final moment in an Old Firm match was a red card – but he contributed to yet another Rangers victory, one which more or less sealed nine-in-a-row on 16 March 1997

Chapter 10
At Home

Ibrox Stadium is now one of the best in the world. A state-of-the-art arena which will soon, again, host major European finals. The work started by Willie Waddell has been taken on with vision by David Murray.

Revolution is a word used too often when describing the remarkable transformation which has taken place at Ibrox in the last 20 years. Change has been at a colossal level, but a look at the first 50 years of the club's history proves even more extraordinary.

Rangers have come a long way from their very first games on the public pitches of Glasgow Green. As the club grew in stature and support, new accommodation was needed and homes at Burnbank and Kinning Park were found suitable – up to a point.

A move was made to Ibrox, where the current Edmiston House stands, but by the end of the century the ground was rapidly becoming inadequate for soaring attendances and the club moved almost adjacent to the present Edmiston Drive site.

Archibald Leitch's architectural legacy

As Rangers grew, so did the stadium, and architect Archibald Leach was commissioned to modernize the grandstand – and the impressive red-brick facade he designed still stands today.

Leitch's stand was different from any other he had built. His trademark criss-cross balcony, which can still be seen at the likes of Everton's Goodison Park and Portsmouth's Fratton Park, was of course central. It was his detail in the interior, though, which was to set Rangers apart from the rest.

The new stand which resulted, the most imposing and impressive in Scotland, was testament to the progression of the club since their first matches in 1872 and formal foundation in 1873.

Leitch decided to ditch the mainstream stadium idea of the bare minimum. As many clubs in Scotland fought for internal space, Rangers were granted huge dressing rooms and capacious offices for personnel. This was also a sign of the club's wealth and prosperity and today it remains almost as it was all those years ago.

Described as a "hotel without rooms", the entrance hall and staircase are resplendent in marble and no expense was spared as art deco lights were installed and costly wooden panels fitted to the walls.

From Ibrox's high stands the game can look so beautiful and so simple

Only recently, much work has taken place to bring back that "old" look with the marble being completely re-laid and the whole interior spruced up. Some of the most impressive rooms, such as the Blue Room, Boardroom and Directors' Room, have been revamped but they still retain the original feel. Much work has been done to ensure that in a day of £20,000 weekly wage payments, Rangers still retain their sense of inherited history.

The stand was completed in 1928 and opened one year later on 1 January by Glasgow's Lord Provost. It joined the old oval-shaped terracing, and it witnessed some mammoth football games. One in particular was the Old Firm clash of 1939 when 118,730 packed into Ibrox, a record which is unlikely ever to be surpassed.

The Ibrox disaster

Whilst fans filled the sweeping terraces week after week, it was terrible human tragedy which was to bring about the ground's downfall. In 1971 the Ne'er Day derby witnessed disaster of sickening proportions. In a crush at Stairway 13, 66 supporters lost their lives and 145 were injured.

After such appalling scenes, club manager Willie Waddell ensured a player, or member of Rangers staff, attended each funeral. It was Waddell who also worked tirelessly to upgrade the stadium, and he got his way, albeit seven years later.

Waddell was adamant there was no future for dangerous terracing, crush barriers or hazardous stairways and he took tips from top European sides who already had all-seater stadia in place. The bulldozers hit Ibrox in 1978 and a great part of the club's history, the east terracing, was wiped out.

Reconstruction for the modern age

In its place rose the Copland Road Stand, a modern rectangular-shaped structure, which looked harsh to the eye compared to the old, massive, saucer-shaped terracing. It was quickly accepted, though, and when another two stands were erected – the Broomloan and then the Govan Stand – fans rejoiced in the fact that Ibrox was now Scotland's finest stadium.

Unlike their city rivals at Parkhead, where vast terracing stood for another 15 years, Ibrox had been transformed into a neat, modern stadium with a greater emphasis on safety than ever before. Only the huge enclosure tier underneath Leitch's main stand gave a reminder of the past. The cost of the massive works which had taken place over the years was £10 million.

David Murray unveils the memorial to those who died at the Ibrox disaster

Financing the move was not as simple as nowadays – there was none of David Murray's mint – and the majority of the cash came from the very successful pools organization.

Changes off the field

As much work was done on the ground, there was great change off it as well. The club, owned by Lawrence Marlborough, was growing rapidly, although the success off the field didn't necessarily filter its way on to the pitch. In the 1977–78 season Rangers clinched the League and the domestic treble, but the next time such an honour was to be bestowed on the club was in the 1986–87 season.

It was not until one of Scottish football's most sensational signings took place in April 1986 that Ibrox finally had something to shout about. Graeme Souness arrived with one thought in mind – to bring back the glory days to Ibrox. With a successful career in the superb Liverpool sides of the 1970s and 1980s he had exactly the credentials chairman David Holmes wanted, although possibly it was the experience of Serie A football which made him stand out from the rest.

From the word "go" Souness made the difference. The side started to pick up regular wins and a new breed of player joined the club. With them started to come a new breed of fan as well. Businesses wanted to be associated with success and corporate hospitality became a lucrative prospect.

Individual fans with a greater personal spending power were attracted back to Ibrox, some being attracted to watching football on a live, season-long basis for the first time. The core fans were still single males with a working-class and middle-class background but the spread – women, children, families, corporations, Glasgow Asians – began to change as more and more trophies were won.

Souness, though, also persuaded one other man to join; Edinburgh businessman David Murray. This move would prove to be one of the club's biggest – and best – signings of all time. The new chairman of Rangers parted with £4 million and promised bigger and better things. Murray realized his stadium could be utilized to greater effect. He had a vision of a Blue Heaven – and he delivered.

Blue Heaven

In 1991 the Club Deck Stand was added to Ibrox on top of the listed main stand building, the last surviving terracing was demolished and seats were put in place. That was financed largely by the debenture scheme run by Rangers, where patrons paid a substantial amount of cash to guarantee a seat for life. Such a project was a hit with fans, although it took English counterparts Arsenal for example, a little longer to come round to the idea.

Ibrox is stylish, luxurious and full of reminders of its roots

The whole stadium has now been re-seated – in blue, of course – and the unsightly corners which join the Copland and Broomloan Stands to the Govan Stand have been filled in, boosting the capacity to just under 51,000 on match days. Giant Jumbotron screens have also been put in place in these new corners and these have proved to be a smash hit with the fans, not just on match days.

With Rangers being in a unique situation where no cash has been passed at a turnstile for the last nine seasons, there is much demand to see the team in action.

When the club played Hearts in the last game of the 1996–97 season at Tynecastle, the home of Heart of Midlothian, over 35,000 packed into Ibrox to watch the beam-back match. And, with tickets almost impossible to find for away games, this is one avenue the huge commercial department is tapping into.

Other prestigious occasions

With Hampden Park undergoing renovation and Parkhead also out of action due to redevelopment, Ibrox has been used by the governing bodies for international games and numerous cup ties.

Scotland's charge for the World Cup in France, 1998, was given a great boost when over 40,000 fans packed

Ibrox's ground facade is an architectural landmark in the city of Glasgow

into the ground to see the Dark Blues beat Sweden 1–0. A match against Italy has also been featured at Ibrox and many cup games, including last season's Scottish Cup final between Falkirk and Kilmarnock, have been held here.

Only recently the ground was given the go-ahead for the European Cup-Winners' Cup Final but by a remarkable twist of fate the idea had to be scrapped because there were no hotels available in the city… due to a medical convention. It is the desire of the current Rangers administration to hold such an event at Ibrox in the near future, as that would confirm the club's status with the European game.

The commercial side of the business is now massive. In 1996–97 Rangers were listed as the second most profitable club in Europe, with only English champions Manchester United excelling them. A great deal of United's cash is made through the massive input of television revenue. In Scotland such deals from satellite television are smallfry compared to their English counterparts.

Rangers' wage bill is well over the £10 million mark and turnover each season soars above £30 million. Money from playing in the Champions' League is another bonus for the club – in 1995–96 they received £4.9 million, despite finishing bottom of the League!

Success in Europe would bolster the club's financial status quite considerably.

Like many growing football clubs, the lion's share of money is now found from activities off the park. Gate receipts are now nowhere near what is needed to keep the club afloat. On a match day, the catering side of the commercial wing employs over 500 personnel. Over the season a staggering turnover of £4 million is churned out.

Restaurants, as well as the many fast-food outlets, make sure the stadium is utilized to the maximum. Despite many clubs aiming upmarket for much-needed money, Ibrox proves there is still a lot of cash in pies and Bovril!

Other financial boosts in recent years have come from the many rock concerts which have taken place. Over 50,000 packed in for a Bon Jovi concert and the likes of Rod Stewart and even Frank Sinatra have snubbed some more established venues to play at Ibrox.

Regardless of how much money such ventures pull in, they were nothing compared to the actions of one man in January 1997 when billionaire businessman Joe Lewis pumped £40 million into the club, acquiring a shareholding of over 25%.

Ten years after Murray purchased Rangers for £4 million, a recluse who lives in a Caribbean hideaway commanded a quarter-share for 10 times what the current chairman paid. The deal is the biggest single financial investment ever to have taken place in a British side. Rangers already had respect in footballing circles but this deal certainly put the cat amongst the pigeons.

London-born Lewis is Britain's richest man, and although he made his fortune from the restaurant trade he left the country and extended his incredible wealth on the world's money-markets. Lewis is a man of great intrigue. To anyone's knowledge he has never met Murray and therefore it is highly unlikely he has attended a Rangers game. He is a man who shuns the media and despite living lavishly – he owns a multi-million pound yacht – he tends to keep out of the spotlight.

When his negotiators finally agreed a deal with Murray in his Edinburgh headquarters, it wasn't just Scotland's media that went to town. Across the world this was huge news – but was buying into Rangers Football Club the big story or was HE the main attraction as far as this one went?

Over the years there has been little contact between Lewis and the media, although he did tell *Rangers News*, the club's official paper: "This deal will help Rangers become one of Europe's biggest sides. The potential is here to be exploited." And with an additional £40 million in the coffers Rangers were able to take seriously the prospect of a hotel being built within the ground. A hotel without any rooms? Maybe not ...

Lewis' boost confirms the marketability of Rangers. When the Govan Stand was completed in the early 1980s crowds of under 10,000 were not uncommon. Now the average gate at Ibrox is just under 49,000. The transformation has been remarkable and that, in turn, has attracted a new breed of player such as England's Paul Gascoigne and Denmark's Brian Laudrup.

During the close season (1997–98) Walter Smith stunned British football by snapping up eight new stars. These players were snubbing Italian sides and, more importantly if you were a Rangers fan, English giants Manchester United.

Celebrity Blues

Saturday games at Ibrox now are a veritable Who's Who. Joe Lewis may not be a fan himself but he has lifted the club's prominence to an all-time high. Before, the odd minor celebrity could be spotted within the walls of the stadium, but times have changed.

One of the more well-known actors to attend games here is Sean Connery, of James Bond fame, amongst other roles. Connery, believed to have been brought up a Celtic fan in the Fountainbridge area of Edinburgh, is a close friend of Murray and travels to most European games on the chairman's private jet.

Sean Connery attends many Rangers' matches – some in the chairman's private jet

Other celebs in the shape of golfer Arnold Palmer – who is one of 7,000 shareholders – have a close affinity with the club. Indeed, former broadcaster Alistair Burnett is actually believed to have read the national news sporting his favourite club tie!

Nowadays it is trendy for the glitzy and glamourous to support a club. Only a few years ago this would have been frowned upon, but as the game changes for the new millennium so does the public perception. In the last 10 years clubs have been forced to adapt due to the Taylor Report after the Hillsborough disaster. Rangers, it could be said, have modified more than anyone.

The heart of the club – which has ticked strongly for over 100 years now – is beating even stronger as another era comes along. Another revolution? Perhaps.

Chapter 11
The Other Great Matches

The hype would suggest otherwise, but nine consecutive titles have not been won through Old Firm results alone. Walter Smith has always pointed out that the challenge has varied.

RANGERS 2, ABERDEEN 0
Premier Division
11 May 1991

It was an afternoon when winning titles had still to be taken for granted. An afternoon when thousands stood outside, ticketless, distraught and then delirious. An afternoon when Rangers gave one of the finest performances of their recent history to beat Aberdeen and win the League.

It had built up to a wonderful climax when Alex Smith's side pushed their long unbeaten spell right up to this, the last

**RANGERS 2
ABERDEEN 0 (ht 1 – 0)**

Rangers:
Woods; Stevens, Cowan, Nisbet, Spackman, Brown, Hurlock, Ferguson, Hateley, Johnston, Walters. Subs: Durrant McCoist

Aberdeen:
Watt; Wright, Grant, Robertson, McLeish, McKimmie, Vande Ven, Bett, Jess, Connor, Gillhaus. Subs: Van der Ark, Booth

HT 1–0 FT 2–0

Rangers scorer: Hateley (2)
Attendance: 37,652

The performance of his life – Hateley's second goal, the League clincher, against Aberdeen

game of the season, and Rangers nose-dived the previous week at Motherwell.

Souness had departed, dramatically, a matter of weeks before and Walter Smith's side was a collection of the injured, the half-fit and the out of position.

John Brown played when it was ludicrous to do so, Gough was in hospital, Durrant and McCoist played but would not have done so in normal circumstances. Walters played on in pain, Tom Cowan broke his leg and Brown picked up a long-term injury. By the end, even Hateley, McCoist and Hurlock were playing as defenders but still Rangers won 2–0.

Walters' cross after 39 minutes was brilliantly headed past Watt by Hateley and after Peter van de Ven and Hans Gilhaus had both missed opportunities for Aberdeen, Hateley added another when Mo Johnston's shot was only parried by Watt.

Without any doubt this was the victory which imbued the entire club with a belief that anything was possible – even nine in a row.

ABERDEEN 2, RANGERS 3
Premier Division
4 December 1991

More than simply being the second in a 16-game undefeated run, this was an antidote to both a recent 0–1 loss to St Mirren and another to Aberdeen at home in Ibrox.

Hearts were League leaders and neither team could really afford to miss this chance to close the gap after the Edinburgh side faltered against Falkirk.

It was an absolutely superb game, pushed to its thrilling climax when the home side equalized rather improbably after Rangers had established dominance and twice taken the lead.

McCoist and Hateley's good work created a shooting chance for Dale Gordon, but Theo Snelders did well to save. When the ball dropped ten yards out, Hateley simply followed up to smash it home and Rangers were ahead within five minutes.

Just over 60 seconds later, Gilhaus was fouled in the box by Gary Stevens and the Dutchman took the kick, hit the post and watched as his team mate Theo Ten Caat poked in the rebound.

The pearl of the evening preceded half time. McCoist did some assiduous defensive work and found Hateley in his own half with a clearance.

The Englishman peeled away from David Winnie, played a one-two with Stuart McCall and simply destroyed the Aberdeen defender for pace before scoring majestically from 15 yards out.

Just after the hour it looked like a comfortable win for the champions when Robertson found Hateley leaping up to knock the ball on for McCoist.

His finish was from the top drawer and gave Rangers a lead 3–1 but a Hateley mistake, ironically, let Gilhaus intercept and from Goram's rebound, Irvine scored to make the finish tight – but it was Rangers' night.

ABERDEEN 2
RANGERS 3 (ht 1–2)

Rangers:
Goram; Stevens, Robertson, Gough, Spackman, Kuznetsov, Gordon, McCall, McCoist, Hateley, Mikhailichenko
Subs: Brown, Durrant

Aberdeen:
Snelders; Kane, Winnie, Cameron, McLeish, Irvine, Van de Ven, Bett, Van der Ark, Ten Caat, Gilhaus
Subs: Jess, Booth
HT 1–2 FT 2–3

Rangers scorers:
Hateley (2), McCoist.

Aberdeen scorers:
Ten Caat, Irvine.

Hateley celebrates after sprinting half the pitch, leaving Aberdeen defenders in his wake, and scoring a marvellous goal in December 1991

RANGERS 4, RAITH ROVERS 0
Premier Division
16 April 1994

Drama and quality in almost equal measure as Rangers turned on the style to thrash Raith but Duncan Ferguson sparked the start of his departure from Scotland with an incident which caused an absolute furore for months.

Ferguson's immense price tag, over £4 million, was undoubtedly weighing heavily on his young shoulders by the time he scored his first goal for the club – something which was betrayed by his foolish headbutt in the direction of John McStay.

Everyone in the crowd expected him to receive a card, probably red, but that didn't come until he was booked for over-celebrating his goal after his smart little dink over Scott Thomson.

By then it was 3–0 and party mode had kicked in but in the following weeks, Ferguson was to receive a ban, a jail term and his marching orders from Rangers – it was just one of those things which wasn't meant to be.

Robertson had a smashing match and scored from long range for the first goal before hitting the post a few minutes later. McCoist, too, scored and hit the woodwork – with a chip off the bar.

Mikhailichenko added his own garnish to the party fare before Ferguson cracked one off the post with only nine minutes left.

It was rampant stuff, champagne football, but the hangover followed for big Duncan.

RANGERS 4 (ht 2–0) RAITH ROVERS 0
Rangers: Maxwell; McCall, Gough, Robertson, McPherson, Brown, Durrant, Ferguson, McCoist, Ferguson, Durie. Subs: Hateley, Mikhailichenko
Raith Rovers: Thomson; McStay, Rowbotham, Coyle, Dennis, McGeachie, Nicholl, Graham, Hetherston, Crawford, Lennon
HT 2–0 FT 4–0
Scorers: Robertson, McCoist, Ferguson, Mikhailichenko
Attendance: 42,545

RANGERS 3, HEARTS 0
Premier Division
11 September 1994

No-one would dare say that this was a game when Rangers fired on all cylinders or played with the verve which the team was capable of, but few victories have been as welcome as this one during the nine-title sequence.

It was preceded by three horrible home defeats in a row – to AEK Athens, Celtic and Falkirk in three different competitions.

That would always be bad enough, but so much expectation had followed the arrival of Brian Laudrup and Basile Boli, perhaps an unfair amount, that the early teething troubles were extra sore for Rangers.

Before the game, Hateley was presented with a golden boot award in recognition of his 30 goals the previous season and naturally enough this was all the inspiration the Englishman needed.

Tension grew in the first half when no damage was done to a Hearts team which hadn't won and had only scored twice that season.

But Laudrup put things on course with a driving run which put Hateley in the box only for Henry Smith to bring him down.

The penalty was scored, nervelessly, and with it went the game.

Hearts' nerve was broken and Rangers relaxed into a passing frame of mind which allowed Laudrup, again, to feed Hateley for 2–0.

From Robertson's cross with 15 minutes left the hat trick seemed on but Durie was better positioned, Hateley let the ball go and Durie's low header hit the back of the net.

The temporary rot was stopped and this became Championship number seven.

RANGERS 3 HEARTS 0 (ht 0–0)
Rangers: Goram; McCall, Robertson, Gough, McPherson, Moore, Murray, Ferguson I, Durrant, Hateley, Laudrup. Subs Durie, Ferguson D
Hearts: Smith; Locke, McKinlay, Levein, Berry, McLaren, Calquhoun, Leitch, Johnston, Millar, Robertson
HT 0–0 FT 3–0
Rangers scorers: Hateley (2), Durie
Attendance: 41,041

MOTHERWELL 1, RANGERS 3
Premier Division
31 December 1994

When Walter Smith looks back on his achievements it will be a group of matches like this one which give him great satisfaction – at a job done well under great pressure.

This win moved Rangers to a remorseless ten points ahead of the pack but it was done with Motherwell pushing them hard on both industry and quality – had it not been for Laudrup, Miodrag Krivokapic would have been the classiest man on the pitch.

So often the tale of Rangers is the story of Laudrup and on this important evening it was the same.

He not only twisted and turned Motherwell so that Alex McLeish's players could never turn competitiveness into dominance but also compensated for the absence of McCoist and Hateley.

Shaun McSkimming had hit the post just before Rangers took the lead and removed some of the pressure.

Laudrup and Huistra helped the build-up but it was McCall, with his first league goal for six months, who provided the finish.

After the interval, Laudrup jinked his way off the left touchline and curled the ball beyond Stevie Woods. It hit the post and rebounded off the keeper's body into the empty net for a slapstick end to some Danish magic.

Before that, Motherwell had equalized when McSkimming's pass sent McGrillen through to score with a low, accurate shot past Colin Scott.

The policy of using two wingers paid off when Huistra curved an exhilerating pass to Durie for the striker to nip around Woods and stroke home the third.

It was good, heart-warming football in the depth of winter with a difficult Old Firm derby approaching. The ten point cushion was eaten into but never sufficiently and it was away wins like this that helped bring title number seven.

RANGERS 7, HIBERNIAN 0
Premier Division
30 December 1995

Only a year later something important had changed about Rangers. Certainly the game was at home but the Laudrup and Gascoigne connection had sparked and suddenly Rangers were a team which didn't "only" win vital championship matches – they were a team which could utterly demolish opponents who didn't need to do too much to help their own downfall.

What will often be overlooked, in retrospect, is that Rangers were in the midst of playing 11 important games in less than two months, while pitches and weather were at their worst and injuries combined with suspension to make consistant team selection difficult. The last time Alex Miller had taken his team to Ibrox Hibs played with stuffy obstinance and a Darren Jackson penalty gave them a shock win – not something which was ever on the cards this time.

The first goal was far from the most spectacular of the bunch but it was still wonderfully taken by

---

**MOTHERWELL 1
RANGERS 3 (ht 0 – 1)**

Rangers:
Scott; McCall, Robertson, Gough, McLaren, McPherson, Huistra, Ferguson, Durie, Laudrup. Sub: Pressley

Motherwell:
Woods; Shannon, McSkimming, Philliben, Krivokapic, McCart, Lambert, McSkimming, Coyne, Arnett, Davies
HT 0–1 FT 1–3

Rangers scorers:
McCall, Laudrup, Durie.
Motherwell scorers:
McGrillen
Attendance: 11,500

Gazza scores in one of the best displays of the nine championships – 7–0 vs Hibs in 1995

**RANGERS 7
HIBERNIAN 0 (ht 0 – 1)**

Rangers:
Goram; Cleland, Robertson, Gough, McLaren, Petric, Miller, Durie, Salenko, Gascoigne Laudrup

Hibs:
Leighton; Miller, Tortukno, McGinlay, Tweed, Hunter, McAllister, C. Jackson, Wright, D. Jackson, Weir
Sub: Harper
HT 1–0 FT 7–0

Rangers scorers:
Durie (4), Salenko, Gascoigne, Miller
Attendance: 44,392

Charlie Miller, on the half hour, as he curled a pass from Gordon Durie elegantly past Jim Leighton.

The Scottish international goalie, throughout his long career, has often taken great pleasure from being the one to deny Rangers but this was an afternoon which was to leave him distraught – an hour after Miller's opening goal, Leighton was leaving the pitch and continuously shaking his head as if he could not believe what had just taken place.

Gordon Durie was the quickest of the Rangers players to sense that something special was on and he connected at the back post for 2–0 after Laudrup had woven a little bit of his own magic on the touchline.

After half time Hibs played as if Miller's words had stung them but when Durie's effort at goal took a nice little clip off a defender to spiral over Leighton a lot of the men in green just chucked it.

The *piece de resistance* – of the first half of the season – not just the match, came when Paul Gascoigne decided he needed to stamp his own personality on the afternoon.

Taking the ball up in an unthreatening area he turned Gordon Hunter, threaded the ball past a multitude of dumbfounded Hibs players and eased the ball beyond Jim Leighton. It was a run worthy of Maradona and a finish made by Jimmy Greaves.

Durie made his hat-trick two minutes later and Oleg Salenko got in on the act for 6–0.

Five minutes before the end Durie became the first player since January 1987 to score four goals in a Premier League match.

Walter Smith called it: "as good a 90 minutes as we have ever turned in" while Alex Miller, back at the ground where he made his career, said: "This has been the most embarrassing day of my life – this defeat is the biggest of my career."

RANGERS 3, ABERDEEN 1
Premier Division
28 April 1996

This was the definitive Gascoigne match and surely the classiest way to win a title. The rivalry between the two teams in recent years added an extra piquancy to the victory but also made the beginning of the game a nervy affair In the previous game at Ibrox, Roy Aitken's side played with organization and grit. Championships had regularly been won against Aberdeen, dating back to Souness's first, and the fans

Gazza '96: It's great, it's eight, and everyone's me mate

expected nothing more than a token presence from the visitors, but nerves took something from Rangers' early moves and Aberdeen took the lead.

Glass' corner dropped where no-one was able to defend it adequately and Brian Irvine, who had just rejoined play after a head injury, shot past Goram.

Had it taken long for Rangers to fight back the nerves would inevitably have bitten harder but Gascoigne scored one of the best goals of his career just over a minute later to equalize and the match was never going wrong from that point.

McCall fed him and Gascoigne dragged the ball past three Aberdeen players before changing body stance, opening the goal up with the movement and using the side of his foot to send a rising drive past Watt.

McLaren hit the post with a header from McCall's chip and then the same defender met a corner kick full on but Watt pushed the ball onto the bar.

Aberdeen had never given up but the match increasingly demanded a result – it just was not an afternoon which was meant to be inconclusive.

Nine minutes were left when Gascoigne picked the ball up around the half way line. He seemed to know what was going to happen as he sped away from Paul Bernard and cut past the red shirts which tried to block the

---

**RANGERS 3
ABERDEEN 1 (ht 1 – 1)**

Rangers:
Goram; Steven, Robertson, Gough, McLaren, Brown, Durie, Gascoigne, Andersen, McCall, Laudrup. Subs: Durrant, McCoist, Petric

Aberdeen:
Watt; McKimmie, Smith, Rowson, Irvine, Inglish, Bernard, Windass, Booth, Dodds, Glass. Subs: Grant, Sitllie, Kpedekpo

HT 1–1 FT 3–1

Rangers scorers:
Gascoigne (3).

Aberdeen scorer:
Irvine

Attendance: 47,247

path to goal.

His run ended with a brilliant, curving left-foot shot which bulged the net and sent the crowd wild.

For the match to become truly irreplaceable as 'Gazza's Game' a hat-trick was required and so a hat-trick was provided.

Laudrup sent Durie free but he was pulled down by Barnard in the area. McCoist was told in "industrial language" that only one man was taking the penalties that day. Gascoigne scored from the spot with the easy confidence which only the truly talented can manage. It was one of the finest individual performances in Scotland in a quarter of a century.

RANGERS 6, DUNFERMLINE 1
Premier Division
22 October 1996

This Coca-Cola Cup semi-final would not class as a great match by the normal criteria – the level of competition was too low for that, but a couple of the goals scored in this game were absolutely top drawer, and merit the match with inclusion in this chapter.

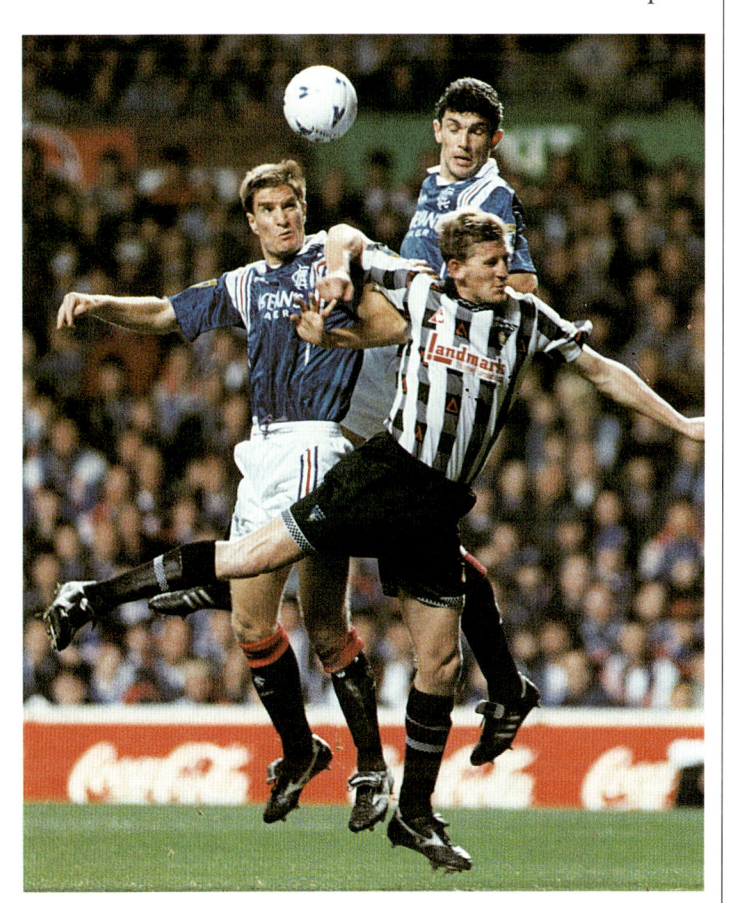

There can be only one – Richard Gough during Rangers' 6–1 thrashing of Dunfermline

Rangers had too often struggled in preceding years to utterly impose themselves in games like this, which should have ended with scores closer to those of cricket, rather than football. This time they did not miss out on goals aplenty.

A defeat and a draw in the League preceded this semi-final, results which brings pressure on a club like Rangers – especially when a loss had not even been contemplated at Parkhead.

But this venue, as a neutral ground for Cup ties, had often been eminently fertile for Rangers and so it was to prove once more.

The game began in a fairly straightforward manner, and the only spruce move of the first half gave Rangers the lead when Gascoigne's simple-looking shimmy gave him the space and the time to feed the ball through to Albertz on the run. The German laid the ball up for Laudrup who scored easily.

Derek McInnes added the second midway through the second half but then Dunfermline briefly sparked a fightback with Andy Smith's shot, which bounced off Snelders only for Allan Moore follow up on the rebound.

What was special and curious about this match was that from being only 2–1 up in the second half of the game, with possible problems looming as their opposition seemed to be making a comeback, Rangers suddenly sped away to a 6–1 win.

Laudrup was the catalyst – he sent McInnes in for another shot which substitute Erik Bo Andersen deflected past Lemajic, and then the Dane scored a vicious second goal only two minutes later when he skillfully pushed the ball past Tod and let rip with a prodigious shot.

Laudrup then scored a goal of a much higher class. He left half the Dunfermline team in his wake as he made the score 5–1 to Rangers, and then another bit of space-conjuring by Gascoigne allowed Albertz, so instrumental in the making of the first goal, to power home his own goal: number six.

**RANGERS 6 (ht 1–0)
DUNFERMLINE 1**

Rangers:
Snelders; Cleland, Robertson, Gough, Petric, Bjorklund, McInnes, Gascoigne, Andersen, Albertz, Laudrup. Subs: Durrant, Moore, Shields

Dunfermline:
Lemajic; Miller, Millar, Den Bieman, Clark, Tod, Moore, Robertson, Smith, French, Petrie. Subs: Britton, Fleming, Westwater.

HT 1–0 FT 6–1

Rangers scorers:
Laudrup (2) Andersen (2) McInnes, Albertz
Dunfermline scorer:
Moore
Attendance: 16,791

Chapter 12
The Records
Year-by-year statistics
Season 1988–89

PREMIER DIVISION

Date	Opponent	Venue	Att	Score	Scorers
13 Aug	Hamilton	A	10,500	2–0	Stevens, McCoist
20 Aug	Hibernian	H	41,955	0–0	
27 Aug	Celtic	H	42,858	5–1	McCoist (2), Wilkins, Drinkell, Walters
3 Sep	Motherwell	A	20,112	2–0	Drinkell, Durrant
17 Sep	Hearts	A	25,501	2–1	Durrant (pen), Nisbet
24 Sep	St Mirren	H	35,523	2–1	D Cooper (pen), Walters
27 Sep	Dundee U	A	20,071	1–0	I Ferguson
1 Oct	Dundee	H	40,768	2–0	Drinkell, Walters
8 Oct	Aberdeen	A	23,370	1–2	N Cooper
12 Oct	Hibernian	A	26,000	1–0	McCoist
29 Oct	St Mirren	A	20,903	1–1	Gray
1 Nov	Hearts	H	36,505	3–0	Gough, Walters (pen), Gray
5 Nov	Motherwell	H	36,060	2–1	Brown, Drinkell
12 Nov	Celtic	A	60,113	1–3	Walters
16 Nov	Hamilton	H	33,864	3–1	Gray, I Ferguson, Drinkell
19 Nov	Dundee	A	16,514	0–0	
26 Nov	Aberdeen	H	42,239	1–0	Gough
3 Dec	Dundee U	H	39,123	0–1	
10 Dec	Hearts	A	26,424	0–2	
17 Dec	Hibernian	H	36,672	1–0	McCall
31 Dec	Hamilton	A	10,500	1–0	D Ferguson
3 Jan	Celtic	H	42,515	4–1	Walters (2) (1 pen), Butcher, Ferguson
7 Jan	Motherwell	A	19,275	1–2	Drinkell
14 Jan	Aberdeen	A	23,000	2–1	Munro, D Ferguson
21 Jan	Dundee	H	43,202	3–1	I Ferguson, Butcher, McCoist
11 Feb	Dundee U	A	22,019	1–1	Munro
25 Feb	St Mirren	H	39,021	3–1	I Ferguson, McCoist, Walters
11 Mar	Hamilton	H	35,733	3–0	I Ferguson, Sterland, Gough
25 Mar	Hibernian	A	23,321	1–0	Drinkell
1 April	Celtic	A	60,171	2–1	Drinkell, I Ferguson
8 April	Motherwell	H	33,782	1–0	McCoist
22 April	St Mirren	A	22,096	2–0	I Ferguson, McCoist
29 April	Hearts	H	42,856	4–0	Sterland (2), Drinkell (2)
2 May	Dundee U	H	39,068	2–0	Drinkell, McCoist
6 May	Dundee	A	14,889	2–1	Gray (2)
13 May	Aberdeen	H	42,480	0–3	

Position: Champions

PLAYER RECORDS (TOTAL)

Name	App	Subs	Goals
Woods, C	39		0
Stevens	52		2
Munro	31	(+3)	2
Gough	51		4
Wilkins	43	(+2)	2
Butcher	51		4
Drinkell	47		19
Brown	41	(+1)	3
McCoist	31	(+2)	18
Durrant	14		4
Walters	48	(+1)	17
Ferguson D	18	(+6)	3
Cooper D	12	(+20)	1
Souness	0	(+10)	
Ferguson I	43		13
Nisbet	6	(+4)	2
Gray 3 (+13)	5		
Cooper N	14	(+3)	1
Walker	13		0
McDonald	2	(+1)	0
McCall	2	(+5)	1
McSwegan	0	(+1)	0
Nicholl	3		0
Cowan	3	(+1)	0
Sterlan d	11	(+2)	3
Kirkwood	2		0
Robertson A	1	(+1)	0
McGregor	0	(+1)	0

Season 1988–89

LEAGUE CUP

Date	Team	Venue	Att	Score	Scorer
2nd Round					
17 Aug	Clyde	A	14,699	3–0	Drinkell, Walters, D Ferguson
3rd Round					
24 Aug	Clydebank	H	34,376	6–0	McCoist, Gough, Walters, Wilkins, Drinkell, Durrant
Quater-final					
31 Aug	Dundee	H	39,667	4–1	McCoist (pen), Walters, I Ferguson, Forsyth (og)
Semi-final					
21 Sep	Hearts	N	53,623	3–0	Walters (2), Nisbet
Final					
23 Oct	Aberdeen	N	72,122	3–2	McCoist (2), I Ferguson.

SCOTTISH CUP

Date	Team	Venue	Att	Score	Scorer
3rd Round					
28 Jan	Raith R	A	10,500	1–1	I Ferguson
Replay 1 Feb	Raith R	H	40,307	3–0	Walters, Drinkell, Fraser (og)
4th Round					
18 Feb	Stranraer	H	41,198	8–0	Drinkell (2), Brown (2), McCoist (2), I Ferguson, Walters
Quarter-final					
21 Mar	Dundee U	H	42,177	2–2	Drinkell, McCoist
Replay 27 Mar	Dundee U	A	21,872	1–0	McCoist
Semi-final					
15 April	St Johnstone	N	47,374	0–0	
Replay 18 April	St Johnstone	N	44,205	4–0	Walters, Stevens, Drinkell, McCoist
Final					
20 May	Celtic	N	72,069	0–1	

UEFA CUP

Date	Team	Venue	Att	Score	Scorer
1st Round					
7 Sep	Katowice	H	41,120	1–0	Walters
5 Oct	Katowice	A	40,100	4–2	Butcher (2), Durrant, I Ferguson
2nd Round					
26 Oct	Cologne	A	42,587	0–2	
9 Nov	Cologne	H	42,204	1–1	Drinkell

Terry Butcher and and some of the Rangers team celebrating with the League Cup following their Championship win at the end of the 1988–89 season

Season 1989–90

PREMIER DIVISION

Date	Opponent	Venue	Att	Score	Scorers
12 Aug	St Mirren	H	39,951	0–1	
19 Aug	Hibernian	A	22,500	0–2	
26 Aug	Celtic	A	54.000	1–1	Butcher
9 Sep	Aberdeen	H	40,283	1–0	Johnston
16 Sep	Dundee	H	35,836	2–2	McCoist (2)
23 Sep	Dunfermline	A	17,765	1–1	McCoist
30 Sep	Hearts	H	39,554	1–0	Johnston
3 Oct	Motherwell	A	17,667	0–1	
14 Oct	Dundee U	H	36,062	2–1	Johnston, McCoist
25 Oct	St Mirren	A	15,130	2–0	McCoist, Johnston
28 Oct	Hibs	H	35,260	3–0	McCoist (2), Johnston (pen)
4 Nov	Celtic	H	41,598	1–0	Johnston
18 Nov	Dundee	A	14,536	2–0	Johnston, Walters
22 Nov	Aberdeen	A	22,500	0–1	
25 Nov	Dunfermline	H	39,131	3–0	Johnston, Butcher, McCoist
2 Dec	Hearts	A	24,771	2–1	Walters, Steven
9 Dec	Motherwell	H	33,549	3–1	Butcher, McCoist, Brown
16 Dec	Dundee U	A	15,947	1–1	Johnston
23 Dec	St Mirren	H	31,797	1–0	Dodds
30 Dec	Hibernian	A	24,500	0–0	
2 Jan	Celtic	A	54,000	1–0	Spackman
6 Jan	Aberdeen	H	41,351	2–0	Walters, McCoist
13 Jan	Dundee	H	36,993	3–0	McCoist, Dodds, Johnston
27 Jan	Dunfermline	A	17,380	1–0	Stevens
3 Feb	Dundee U	H	39,058	3–1	Walters, McCoist, Johnston
10 Feb	Motherwell	A	17,647	1–1	Johnston
17 Feb	Hearts	H	41,884	0–0	
3 Mar	Dundee	A	12,743	2–2	Johnston, Dodds
17 Mar	St Mirren	A	16,129	0–0	
24 Mar	Hibernian	H	37,542	0–1	
1 Apr	Celtic	H	41,926	3–0	Walters (pen), Johnston, McCoist (pen)
8 Apr	Aberdeen	A	23,000	0–0	
14 Apr	Motherwell	H	39,305	2–1	Steven, Johnston
21 Apr	Dundee U	A	15,995	1–0	Steven
28 Apr	Dunfermline	H	40,769	2–0	McCoist, Dodds
5 May	Hearts	A	20,283	1–1	Munro

Position: Champions

PLAYER RECORDS (TOTAL)

Name	Apps	Subs	Goals
Woods C	37		0
Stevens	44		1
Munro	45		1
Gough	31		0
Wilkins	22		0
Butcher	43		3
Steven	43		5
Ferguson I	28	(+4)	2
McCoist	36	(+2)	18
Johnston	45		17
Walters	36		12
Drinkell	3	(+4)	0
Ferguson D	5	(+3)	0
Ginzburg	8		0
Brown	24	(+3)	2
Nisbet	6	(+3)	0
Cowan	2	(+2)	0
Dodds	4	(+11)	4
Cooper N	2	(+1)	0
McCall	2	(+3)	0
Spackman	23		1
Vinnicombe	1	(+7)	0
Robertson A	(1)		0
Souness	(1)		0
McPherson	(1)		0

The Rangers team celebrating again, this time after their championship win at the end of the 1989–90 season

Season 1990–91

SCOTTISH CUP

Date	Team	Venue	Att	Score	Scorer
3rd Round					
3 Jan	St Johnstone	H	39,003	3–0	Johnston, Brown, Walters
4th Round					
25 Feb	Celtic	A	52,565	0–1	

LEAGUE CUP

Date	Team	Venue	Att	Score	Scorer
2nd Round					
15 Aug	Arbroath	H	31,762	4–0	McCoist 3, I Ferguson
3rd Round					
23 Aug	Morton	A	11,821	2–1	Walters, Pickering (og)
Quater-final					
30 Aug	Hamilton	A	9,162	3–1	Walters (2), Steven
Semi-final					
19 Sep	Dunfermline	N	41,643	5–0	Steven, Johnston, Walters, McCoist, I Ferguson
Final					
22 Oct	Aberdeen	N	61,190	1–2	Walters

EUROPEAN CUP

Date	Team	Venue	Att	Score	Scorer
13 Sep	Bayern M	H	40,253	1–3	Walters (pen)
27 Sep	Bayern M	A	40,000	0–0	

SCOTTISH CUP

Date	Team	Venue	Att	Score	Scorer
3rd Round					
29 Jan	Dunfermline	H	29,003	2–0	Huistra, Spackman
4th Round					
23 Feb	Cowdenbeath	H	29,527	5–0	Hateley (2), Nisbet, McCoist, Walters (pen)
Quarter-final					
17 Mar	Celtic	A	52,286	0–2	

LEAGUE CUP

Date	Team	Venue	Att	Score	Scorer
2nd Round					
21 Aug	East Stirling	H	25,595	5–0	Hateley (2), Steven, Walters, Johnston
3rd Round					
28 Aug	Kilmarnock	H	32,671	1–0	Johnston
Quater-final					
4 Sept	Raith R	H	31,320	6–2	McCoist (3), Butcher, Johnston, Steven
Semi-final					
26 Sept	Aberdeen	N	40,855	1–0	Steven
Final					
28 Oct	Celtic	N	62,817	2–1	Walters, Gough

EUROPEAN CUP

Date	Team	Venue	Att	Score	Scorer
1st Round					
19 Sept	Valletta	A	8,000	4–0	Johnston (2), McCoist (pen), Hateley
2 Oct	Valletta	H	20,627	6–0	Johnston (3) Dodds, Spencer, McCoist
2nd Round					
24 Oct	Red Star Belgrade	A	82,500	0–3	
Nov 7	Red Star Belgrade	H	23,831	1–1	McCoist

118 • The Records

PREMIER DIVISION

Date	Opponent	Venue	Att	Score	Scorers
25 Aug	Dunfermline	H	39,951	3–1	Hateley, Johnston, Walters
1 Sept	Hibernian	A	17,500	0–0	
8 Sept	Hearts	A	22,101	3–1	McCoist (2), Huistra
15 Sept	Celtic	H	38,543	1–1	Hurlock
22 Sept	Dundee U	A	16,270	1–2	Johnston
29 Sept	Motherwell	H	34,863	1–0	Brown
6 Oct	Aberdeen	A	19,500	0–0	
13 Oct	St Mirren	H	38,031	5–0	McCoist (2) (1 pen), Walters (2), Johnston
20 Oct	St Johnstone	A	10,504	0–0	
3 Nov	Hibs	H	35,925	4–0	Hateley (2), Walters, Steven
10 Nov	Dundee U	H	36,995	1–2	McCoist
17 Nov	Motherwell	A	16,457	4–2	Stevens (2), Walters, Johnston
20 Nov	Dunfermline	A	14,480	1–0	Hateley
25 Nov	Celtic	A	52,565	2–1	Johnston, McCoist
1 Dec	Hearts	H	37,623	4–0	Johnston, Hurlock, McCoist, Walters (pen)
8 Dec	St Johnstone	H	34,610	4–1	Walters (2), Johnston (pen), Stevens
15 Dec	St Mirren	A	15,197	3–0	Walters, Johnston (pen), Hateley
22 Dec	Aberdeen	H	37,998	2–2	McCoist (2)
29 Dec	Dundee U	A	17,564	2–1	Johnston, Walters.
2 Jan	Celtic	H	38,399	2–0	Walters, Hateley
5 Jan	Hearts	A	20,956	1–0	Hateley
12 Jan	Dunfermline	H	35,120	2–0	Huistra, Johnston
19 Jan	Hibernian	A	15,500	2–0	Houchen (og), Johnston
9 Feb	St Mirren	H	31,769	1–0	McCoist
16 Feb	Motherwell	H	32,192	2–0	McCoist, Hateley
26 Feb	St Johnstone	A	10,721	1–1	Huistra
2 Mar	Aberdeen	A	22,500	0–1	
9 Mar	Hearts	H	36,128	2–1	Steven, Walters
24 Mar	Celtic	A	52,000	0–3	
30 Mar	Dunfermline	A	14,256	1–0	Stevens
6 Apr	Hibernian	H	35,507	0–0	
13 Apr	St Johnstone	H	35,930	3–0	Durrant, Spencer, Huistra
20 Apr	St Mirren	A	18,473	1–0	A Robertson
24 Apr	Dundee Utd	H	32,397	1–0	Ferguson
4 May	Motherwell	A	17,672	0–3	
11 May	Aberdeen	H	37,652	2–0	Hateley (2)

Position: Champions

PLAYER RECORDS (TOTAL)

Name	Apps	Subs	Goals
Woods C	48		0
Stevens	48		4
Brown	33	(+2)	1
Gough	37		1
Spackman	45		1
Butcher	9		1
Steven	31		5
Ferguson I	13	(+2)	0
Hateley	38	(+4)	15
Johnston	38	(+1)	19
Walters	35	(+4)	15
McCoist	22	(+14)	18
Huistra	16	(+20)	5
Hurlock	34	(+1)	2
Munro	21	0	
Kuznetsov	2	0	
Nisbet	18	(+1)	1
Robertson A	8	(+10)	1
McSwegan	1	(+2)	0
Vinnicombe	11		0
Dodds	5	(+1)	1
Cowan	5	(+2)	0
Spencer	4	(+2)	2
Reid 3		0	
Durrant	3	(+1)	1

Mark Hateley is overjoyed after scoring the first of his two goals against Aberdeen at the end of the 1990–91 season. Rangers were champions again

Season 1991–92

PREMIER DIVISION

Date	Opponent	Venue	Att	Score	Scorers
10 Aug	St Johnstone	H	35,109	6–0	Hateley (3) Johnston (2 pens), Ferguson
13 Aug	Motherwell	H	35,322	2–0	Steven, Maskaant (og)
17 Aug	Hearts	A	22,534	0–1	
24 Aug	Dunfermline	H	35,559	4–0	Huistra, Johnston, Spencer, McCoist
31 Aug	Celtic	A	51,382	2–0	Hateley (2)
7 Sept	Falkirk	A	13,088	2–0	Nisbet, Huistra
14 Sept	Dundee Utd	H	36,347	1–1	McCoist
21 Sept	St Mirren	A	14,503	2–1	Huistra, Nisbet
28 Sept	Aberdeen	H	36,330	0–2	
5 Oct	Airdrie	A	11,101	4–0	McCoist (2), Nisbet, Johnston
8 Oct	Hibernian	H	35,368	4–2	McCoist (2), Huistra, Torolano (og)
12 Oct	St Johnstone	A	10,323	3–2	McCoist (2), Nisbet
19 Oct	Hearts	H	36,481	2–0	McCoist, Mikhailichenko
26 Oct	Falkirk	H	36,441	1–1	Johnston
29 Oct	Dundee Utd	A	15,041	2–3	McCoist(2)
2 Nov	Celtic	H	37,387	1–1	McCoist
9 Nov	Dunfermline	A	13,351	5–0	Gordon (2), Gough, Hateley, McCoist
16 Nov	Airdrie	H	36,934	4–0	Hateley (2), D Robertson, McCoist
19 Nov	Hibernian	A	16,833	3–0	McCoist (2), Hateley
23 Nov	St Mirren	H	386,278	0–1	
30 Nov	Motherwell	A	15,350	2–0	Gordon, Gough
4 Dec	Aberdeen	A	20,081	3–2	Hateley, (2), McCoist
7 Dec	St Johnstone	H	35,784	3–1	Mikhailichenko, Brown, Hateley
14 Dec	Falkirk	A	11,801	3–1	McCoist, Hateley, McCall
21 Dec	Dundee Utd	H	41,448	2–0	McCoist (2)
28 Dec	Dunfermline	H	41,328	2–1	Stevens, Gordon
1 Jan	Celtic	A	51,789	3–1	McCoist, Hateley (pen), Brown
4 Jan	Airdrie	A	12,276	0–0	
11 Jan	Hibernian	H	40,616	2–0	Gordon, McCoist
18 Jan	Motherwell	H	38,217	2–0	McCoist, Mikhailichenko
1 Feb	Hearts	A	24,356	1–0	McCoist
8 Feb	StMirren	A	16,638	2–1	McCoist, Mikhailichenko
25 Feb	Aberdeen	H	38,513	0–0	
29 Feb	Airdrie	H	40,568	5–0	Hateley (3) (2 pens), Brown, Rideout
10 Mar	Hibernian	A	13,387	3–1	Hateley (2) (1 pen), McCoist
14 Mar	Dunfermline	A	12,274	3–1	Mikhailichenko (2), Nisbet
21 Mar	Celtic	H	42, 160	0–2	
28 Mar	St Johnstone	A	9,697	2–1	Hateley (2)
7 Apr	Falkirk	H	36,832	4–1	McCoist (3), Mikhailichenko
11 Apr	Dundee Utd	A	11,713	2–1	Mikhailichenko, Brown.
18 Apr	St Mirren	H	40,362	4–0	McCoist (2), Stevens, Huistra
23 Apr	Motherwell	A	12,515	2–1	Mikhailichenko (2)
28 Apr	Hearts	H	36, 129	1–1	McCoist
2 May	Aberdeen	A	16,580	2–0	McCoist (2)

Position: Champions

PLAYER RECORDS (TOTAL)

Name	Apps	Sub	Goals
Goram	55		0
Stevens	54		2
Robertson D	53		2
Gough	42		3
Spackman	53		1
Nisbet	26		5
Steven	2		1
Ferguson I	17	(+5)	1
Hateley	34	(+1)	23
Johnston	15	(+1)	10
Huistra	31	(+9)	5
Robertson A	3	(+4)	0
Spencer	6	(+5)	1
McCall	44	(+1)	3
Durrant	14	(+6)	1
McCoist	45	(+4)	39
Mikhailichenko	28	(+3)	12
Kuznetsov	17	(+2)	0
Brown	25	(+8)	4
Vinnicombe	1	(+1)	0
McSwegan		(5)	0
McGregor	1		0
Morrow	3		0
Gordon	27	(+1)	5
Rideout	8	(+5)	1
Pressley		(1)	0
Robertson L	1		0

Gary Stevens and Alan McLaren fight it out as Hearts take on Rangers on 1 February 1992

120 • The Records

SCOTTISH CUP

Date	Team	Venue	Att	Score	Scorer
3rd Round					
22 Jan	Aberdeen	A	23,000	1–0	McCoist
4th Round					
15 Feb	Motherwell	H	38,444	2–1	Mikhailichenko (2)
Quarter-final					
3 Mar	St Johnstone	A	10,107	3–0	McCoist, Gough, Hateley
Semi-final					
31 Mar	Celtic	N	45,191	1–0	McCoist
Final					
9 May	Airdrie	N	44,045	2–1	Hateley, McCoist

LEAGUE CUP

Date	Team	Venue	Att	Score	Scorer
2nd Round					
20 Aug	Queen's Park	H	32,230	6–0	Johnston (4), Durrant, Spackman
3rd Round					
28 Aug	Partick Thistle	A	12,587	2–0	Johnston, D Robertson
Quarter-final					
4 Sept	Hearts	A	22,878	1–0	McCoist
Semi-final					
25 Sept	Hibernian	N	40,901	0–1	

EUROPEAN CUP

Date	Team	Venue	Att	Score	Scorer
1st Round					
18 Sept	Sparta Prague	A	11,053	0–1	
2 Oct	Sparta Prague	H	34,260	2–1	McCall (2)

Rough stuff as Rangers take on St Johnstone

Season 1992–93

SCOTTISH CUP

Date	Team	Venue	Att	Score	Scorer
3rd Round					
9 Jan	Motherwell	A	14,314	2–0	McCoist (2)
4th Round					
6 Feb	Ayr United	A	13,176	2–0	McCoist, Gordon
Quarter-final					
6 Mar	Arbroath	A	6,488	3–0	McCoist (pen), Murray, Hateley
Semi-final					
3 Apr	Hearts	N	41,738	2–1	McCoist, MacPherson
Final					
29 May	Aberdeen	N	50,715	2–1	Hateley, Murray

LEAGUE CUP

Date	Team	Venue	Att	Score	Scorer
2nd Round					
11 Aug	Dumbarton	A*	11,091	5–0	Mikhailichenko, McCoist, Hateley, Gordon, Durrant,
3rd Round					
19 Aug	Stranraer	A	4,500	5–0	McCoist (3), Hateley (2)
Quarter-final					
26 Aug	Dundee U	A	15,716	3–2	McCoist, Gough, Huistra
Semi-final					
22 Sept	St Johnstone	N*	30,062	3–1	McCoist
Final					
25 Oct	Aberdeen	N*	45,298	2–1	McCall, Smith (og)

EUROPEAN CUP

Date	Team	Venue	Att	Score	Scorer
1st Round					
16 Sept	Lyngby BK	H	40,036	2–0	Hateley, Huistra
30 Sept	Lyngby BK	A	4,273	1–0	Durrant
2nd Round					
21 Oct	Leeds Utd	H	43,251	2–1	McCoist, Lukic
4 Nov	Leeds Utd	A	25,118	2–1	Hateley, McCoist
Champions' League Group A					
25 Nov	Marseilles	H	41,624	2–2	McSwegan, Hateley
9 Dec	CSKA Moscow	A*	9,000	1–0	Ferguson
3 Mar	Club Brugge KV	A	19,000	1–1	Huistra
17 Mar	Club Brugge KV	H	42,731	2–1	Durrant, Nisbet
7 Apr	Marseilles	A	46,000	1–1	Durrant
21 Apr	CSKA Moscow	H	44,142	0–0	

Season 1992–93

PREMIER DIVISION

Date	Opponent	Venue	Att	Score	Scorers
1 Aug	St Johnstone	H	38,036	1–0	McCoist
4 Aug	Airdrieonians	H	34,613	2–0	Gordon, Hately
8 Aug	Hibernian	A	17,044	0–0	
15 Aug	Dundee	A	12,807	3–4	Ferguson, McCoist (2)
22 Aug	Celtic	H	43,239	1–1	Durrant
29 Aug	Aberdeen	H	41,636	3–1	Mikhailichenko, Durrant, McCoist
2 Sept	Motherwell	A	10,074	4–1	McCoist (3), Brown
12 Sept	Partick Thistle	A	18,460	4–1	MacPherson, McCall, Gough, Hateley
19 Sept	Hearts	H	41,888	2–0	McCall, McCoist
26 Sept	Dundee U	A	13,515	4–0	Huistra (2), McCoist, Steven
3 Oct	Falkirk	H	40,691	4–0	McCoist (4),
7 Oct	St Johnstone	A	9,532	5–1	McCoist (2), Hateley (2), Ferguson
17 Oct	Hibernian	H	40,978	1–0	McCoist,
31 Oct	Motherwell	H	38,719	4–2	McCoist (3) (1 pen), Brown
7 Nov	Celtic	A	51,958	1–0	Durrant
11 Nov	Dundee	H	33,497	3–1	McCoist (2), Hateley
21 Nov	Hearts	A	20,831	1–1	McCoist
28 Nov	Partick Thistle	H	40,939	3–0	Steven, McSwegan, MacPherson
1 Dec	Airdrieonians	A	8,000	1–1	Brown
12 Dec	Falkirk	A	12,000	2–1	Hateley, McCoist
19 Dec	St Johnstone	H	35,369	2–0	D Robertson, Gough
26 Dec	Dundee	A	13,983	3–1	Hateley (2), McCoist
2 Jan	Celtic	H	46,039	1–0	Steven
5 Jan	Dundee Utd	H	40,239	3–2	McCoist, Hateley, McCall
30 Jan	Hibernian	A	17,444	4–3	Hateley (2), Steven, McCoist
2 Feb	Aberdeen	A	15,500	1–0	Hateley
9 Feb	Falkirk	A	34,780	5–0	Steven, Hateley (2), Huistra, D Robertson
13 Feb	Airdrie	H	39,816	2–2	McCoist (2)
20 Feb	Dundee U	A	13,234	0–0	
23 Feb	Motherwell	A	14,006	4–0	Hateley (2), McCoist, Mikhailichenko
27 Feb	Hearts	H	42,128	2–1	McCoist, D Robertson
10 Mar	St Johnstone	A	9,210	1–1	McCoist
13 Mar	Hibernian	H	41,076	3–0	Hateley, McCoist, Hagen
20 Mar	Celtic	A	53,241	1–2	Hateley
27 Mar	Dundee	H	40,294	3–0	McCall, McCoist, Ferguson
30 Mar	Aberdeen	H	44,570	2–0	Ferguson, McCoist
10 Apr	Motherwell	H	41,353	1–0	Brown
14 Apr	Hearts	A	14,622	3–2	Hateley (2), McCall
17 Apr	Partick Thistle	H	42,636	3–1	McSwegan (2), Hagen
1 May	Airdrie	A	11,830	1–0	McSwegan.
4 May	Partick Thistle	A	9,834	0–3	
8 May	Dundee Utd	H	42,917	1–0	Huistra
12 May	Aberdeen	A	13,500	0–1	
15 May	Falkirk	A	8,517	2–1	Mikhailichenko, Hateley

Position: Champions

PLAYER RECORDS (TOTAL)

Name	Apps	Subs	Goals
Goram	52		0
Nisbet	16	(+1)	1
Robertson D	58		3
Gough	39		3
McPherson	53		3
Brownt	57	(+2)	4
Durrant	34	(+13)	7
McCall	53	(+1)	6
McCoist	50	(+2)	49
Hateley	53	(+1)	29
Huistra	37	(+5)	7
Rideout	0	(+1)	0
Kuznetsov	8	(+1)	0
Gordon	22	(+5)	3
Mikhailichenko	24	(+15)	4
Steven	35	(+1)	5
Maxwell	12		0
Ferguson I	42	(+1)	5
Spackman	3	0	
Hagan	6	(+4)	2
Robertson A	0	(+2)	0
Stevens	1	0	
McSwegan	9	(+4)	5
Pressley	8	(+3)	0
Murray	17	(+6)	2
Watson	3	0	
Reid 2			
Robertson L	1	0	

Ally McCoist and Chris Whyte get ready for an incoming corner kick as Leeds take on Rangers in 1992

Season 1993–94

PREMIER DIVISION

Date	Opponent	Venue	Att	Score	Scorers
7 Aug	Hearts	H	43,261	2–1	Hagen, Hateley
14 Aug	St JohnstonA	H	10,152	2–1	Gough, I Ferguson
21 Aug	Celtic	A	47,942	0–0	
28 Aug	Kilmarnock	H	44,243	1–2	Pressley
4 Sept	Dundee	A	14,211	1–1	Hateley
11 Sept	Partick Thistle	H	40,988	1–1	Hateley
18 Sept	Aberdeen	A	19,138	0–2	
25 Sept	Hibernian	H	43,200	2–1	Steven, Hateley
2 Oct	Raith Rovers	A	8,161	1–1	Hetherston (og)
6 Oct	Motherwell	H	39,816	1–2	I Ferguson
9 Oct	Dundee Utd	A	11,262	3–1	Hateley, Huistra (2)
16 Oct	St Johnstone	H	41,960	2–0	Huistra, Hateley
30 Oct	Celtic	H	47,522	1–2	McCoist,
3 Nov	Hearts	A	18,370	2–2	Hateley
6 Nov	Kilmarnock	A	19,162	2–0	I Ferguson, Huistra, Durrant
10 Nov	Dundee	H	38,477	3–1	McCoist (2 pen), I Ferguson
13 Nov	Raith Rovers	H	42,611	2–2	Hateley (2)
20 Nov	Hibernian	A	16,506	1–0	Gough
27 Nov	Partick Thistle	A	17,292	1–1	Huistra
1 Dec	Aberdeen	H	45,182	2–0	Hateley (2)
4 Dec	Motherwell	A	14,069	2–0	Durie (2)
11 Dec	Dundee U	H	43,058	0–3	
18 Dec	St Johnstone	A	10,056	4–0	Hateley (2), Durie, Steven
27 Dec	Hearts	H	45,116	2–2	Hateley (2)
1 Jan	Celtic	A	48,506	4–2	Mikhailichenko (2), Hateley, Kuznetsov
8 Jan	Kilmarnock	H	44,919	3–0	Hateley (2), Huistra
15 Jan	Dundee	A	11,014	1–1	Durie
22 Jan	Aberdeen	A	20,267	0–0	
5 Feb	Partick Thistle	H	42,606	5–1	Durie (2), Mikhailichenko, McCall, Steven
12 Feb	Hibernian	H	43,265	2–0	Durie, Steven
26 Feb	Raith Rovers	A	8,988	2–1	I Ferguson, Durie
5 Mar	Motherwell	H	43,669	2–1	Durie, Hateley (pen)
19 Mar	St Johnstone	H	43,228	4–0	McCall, Hateley, McPherson, Durie
26 Mar	Hearts	A	18,108	2–1	McCoist, Hateley
29 Mar	Partick Thistle	A	14,706	2–1	Gough, McCoist
2 Apr	Aberdeen	H	45,888	1–1	McCall
5 Apr	Dundee U	A	11,353	0–0	
16 Apr	Raith Rovers	H	42,545	4–0	D Robertson, McCoist, D Ferguson, Mikhailichenko
23 Apr	Dundee U	H	44,776	2–1	Durie (2)
26 Apr	Motherwell	A	14,050	1–2	McCoist
30 Apr	Celtic	H	47,018	1–1	Mikhailichenko
3 May	Hibernian	A	14,517	0–1	
7 May	Kilmarnock	A	18,012	0–1	
14 May	Dundee	H	41,629	0–0	

Position: Champions

PLAYER RECORDS (TOTAL)

Name	Apps	Subs	Goals
Maxwell	42	(+1)	0
McCall	44		3
Wishart	8	(+2)	
Robertson D	43		6
Gough	48		3
Pressley	22	(+7)	1
Brown	28		1
Murray	25	(+2)	
Ferguson I	47		9
Hagen	6	(+2)	1
Hateley	53	(+2)	30
Mikhailichenko	28	(+12)	5
Durrant	22	(+9)	2
Huistra	13	(+13)	6
Steven	42		6
Vinnicombe	3	(+2)	
McPherson	36	(+1)	3
Ferguson D	9	(+7)	1
Stevens	36	(+1)	
Kuznetsov	4	(+2)	1
Morrow	14	(+1)	
Miller	2	(+1)	
McCoist	20	(+8)	11
Durie	28	(+1)	13
Scott	5	(+1)	
Goram	10		
Moore	1		

Season 1993–94

SCOTTISH CUP

Date	Team	Venue	Att	Score	Scorer
3rd Round					
29 Jan	Dumbarton	H	36,809	4–1	Durie, Hateley Steven, D Robertson
4th Round					
19 Feb	Alloa Athletic	H	37,804	6–0	McCoist (3) Ferguson I, McPherson, Newbiggin (og)
Quarter-final					
12 Mar	Hearts	H	41,666	2–0	Brown, Hateley
Semi-final					
10 Apr	Kilmarnock	N*	35,144	0–0	
Replay 13 Apr	Kilmarnock	N*	29,860	2–1	Hateley (2)
Final					
21 May	Dundee U	N*	37,450	0–1	

LEAGUE CUP

Date	Team	Venue	Att	Score	Scorer
2nd Round					
11 Aug	Dumbarton	H	36,309	1–0	I Ferguson
3rd Round					
25 Aug	Dunfermline A A		12,993	2–0	Steven, I Ferguson
Quarter-final					
1 Sept	Aberdeen	H	45,604	2–1	Hateley (pen), I Ferguson
Semi-final					
22 Sept	Celtic	H	47,420	1–0	Hateley
Final					
24 Oct	Hibernian	N*	47,632	2–1	McCoist, Durrant

EUROPEAN CUP

Date	Team	Venue	Att	Score	Scorer
1st Round					
15 Sept	Levski Sofia	H	37,013	3–2	Hateley, McPherson
29 Sept	Levski Sofia	A	50,000	1–2	Durrant

Duncan Ferguson chasing hard as Celtic and Rangers meet for an Old Firm clash in 1993

Season 1994–95

PREMIER DIVISION

Date	Opponent	Venue	Att	Score	Scorers
13 Aug	Motherwell	H	43,750	2–1	Hateley, D Ferguson
20 Aug	Partick Thistle	A	15,030	2–0	Hateley, Byrne (og)
27 Aug	Celtic	H	45,466	0–2	
11 Sept	Hearts	H	41,041	3–0	Hateley (2), Durie
17 Sept	Falkirk	A	12,500	2–0	Boli, Laudrup
24 Sept	Aberden	A	21,000	2–2	Hateley, Moore
1 Oct	Dundee Utd	H	43,030	2–0	Hateley, Laudrup
8 Oct	Hibernian	A	12,118	1–2	Boli
15 Oct	Kilmarnock	H	44,099	2–0	Miller, D Robertson
22 Oct	Motherwell	A	11,160	1–2	Philliben (og)
30 Oct	Celtic	A	32,171	3–1	Hateley (2), Laudrup
5 Nov	Partick Thistle	H	43,696	3–0	Miller, Hateley, Laudrup
9 Nov	Hearts	A	12,347	1–1	Hateley
19 Nov	Falkirk	H	44,018	1–1	Hateley
25 Nov	Aberdeen	H	45,072	1–0	McCoist
4 Dec	Dundee Utd	A	10,692	3–0	Laudrup, Huistra, Durrant
10 Dec	Kilmarnock	A	17,283	2–1	McLaren, Laudrup
26 Dec	Hibernian	H	44,892	2–0	Hateley, Gough
31 Dec	Motherwell	A	11,500	3–1	McCall, Laudrup, Durie
4 Jan	Celtic	H	45,794	1–1	I Ferguson
7 Jan	Partick Thistle	A	19,351	1–1	D Robertson
14 Jan	Falkirk	A	13,495	3–2	Huistra (2) (1 pen), McCall
21 Jan	Hearts	H	44,231	1–0	Miller
4 Feb	Dundee Utd	H	44,197	1–1	D Robertson
12 Feb	Aberdeen	A	20,000	0–2	
25 Feb	Kilmarnock	H	44,859	3–0	Durie, Laudrup, Durrant
4 Mar	Hibernian	A	12,059	1–1	McCall
11 Mar	Falkirk	H	43,359	2–2	Brown, Laudrup
18 Mar	Hearts	A	9,806	1–2	Laudrup
1 Apr	Dundee Utd	A	11,500	2–1	Durie, McLaren
8 Apr	Aberdeen	H	44,460	3–2	Durrant, Murray, Hateley
16 Apr	Hibernian	H	44,193	3–1	Durie, Durrant, Mikhailichenko
20 Apr	Kilmarnock	A	16,086	1–0	Mikhailichenko
29 Apr	Motherwell	H	43,576	0–2	
7 May	Celtic	A	31,025	0–3	
13 May	Partick Thistle	H	45,280	1–1	Moore

Position: Champions

PLAYER RECORDS (TOTAL)

Name	Apps	Subs	Goals
Goram	21	(+1)	0
Murray	15	(+7)	1
Robertson D	20		3
Gough	31		1
Boli 31; 3 goals			
McPherson	12		0
Durrant	18	(+13)	4
McCall	36		4
McCoist	4	(+5)	1
Hateley	28		5
Laudrup	38		3
Ferguson D	3	(+4)	4
Brown	11	(+5)	1
Moore	23	(+2	2
Ferguson I	17	(+3)	1
Pressley	3		0
Durie	21	(+6)	
Mikhailichenko	4	(+5)	2
Miller	23	(+0)	3
Huistra	15		3
Hagan		(+2)	
Wishart	3	(+1)	
Mclaren	25		2
Scott	3	(+1)	0
McGinty	1		
Maxwell	13	(+1)	0
Steven	12	(+1)	1
Bollan	5	(+1)	0
Cleland	11		0
Thomson	5		0
Robertson L		(+1)	
Caldwell	1		

SCOTTISH CUP

Date	Team	Venue	Att	Score	Scorer
3rd Round					
6 Feb	Hamilton A	A	18,379	3–1	Steven, Boli, Laudrup
4th Round					
20 Feb	Hearts	A	12,375	2–4	Laudrup, Durie

LEAGUE CUP

Date	Team	Venue	Att	Score	Scorer
2nd Round					
17 Aug	Arbroath	A	4,665	6–1	D Ferguson (3), Hateley (2), McCall
3rd Round					
31 Aug	Falkirk	H	40,697	1–2	Laudrup

EUROPEAN CUP

Date	Team	Venue	Att	Score	Scorer
1st Round					
10 Aug	AEK Athens	A	30,000	0–2	
24 Aug	AEK Athens	H	44,789	0–1	

Season 1995–96

PREMIER DIVISION

Date	Opponent	Venue	Att	Score	Scorers
26 Aug	Kilmarnock	H	44,686	1–0	McCall
9 Sept	Raith Rovers	H	43,284	4–0	McCoist (2), Miller, Robertson
16 Sept	Falkirk	A	11,480	2–0	Salenko, Robertson
23 Sept	Hibernian	H	44,221	0–1	
30 Sept	Celtic	A	33,296	2–0	Cleland, Gascoigne
3 Oct	Motherwell	H	39,891	2–1	Gascoigne, McCoist
7 Oct	Aberdeen	A	20,351	1–0	Moore
14 Oct	Partick Thistle	A	16,066	4–0	Gough, Durie (3)
21 Oct	Hearts	H	45,155	4–1	Gascoigne, Salenko (2), Durie
28 Oct	Raith Rovers	A	9,300	2–2	Gough, Petric
4 Nov	Falkirk	H	42,059	2–0	McCoist (2)
8 Nov	Kilmarnock	A	14,613	2–0	McLaren, Salenko
11 Nov	Aberdeen	H	45,427	1–1	Salenko
19 Nov	Celtic	H	46,640	3–3	Laudrup, McCoist, McKinlay (o.g.)
25 Nov	Hibernian	A	13,558	4–1	McCoist, Dods (o.g.), Miller, Durie
2 Dec	Hearts	A	15,105	2–0	McCoist, Gascoigne
9 Dec	Partick Thistle	H	43,137	1–0	Durie
19 Dec	Motherwell	A	10,197	0–0	
26 Dec	Kilmarnock	H	45,143	3–0	Salenko, Durie (pen), Gascoigne
30 Dec	Hibernian	H	44,692	7–0	Miller, Durie (4), Gascoigne, Salenko
2 Jan	Celtic	A	36,719	0–0	
6 Jan	Falkirk	A	10,348	4–0	Durie, McCoist (2, 1 pen), Robertson
13 Jan	Raith Rovers	H	42,498	4–0	McCoist, Durie (2), Ferguson
20 Jan	Hearts	H	45,096	0–3	
3 Feb	Partick Thistle	A	16,488	2–1	Gascoigne (2)
10 Feb	Motherwell	H	44,871	3–2	Ferguson, McLaren, McCoist (pen)
25 Feb	Aberdeen	A	19,842	1–0	Gascoigne (pen)
3 Mar	Hibernian	A	11,923	2–0	Mitchell (o.g.), Laudrup (pen)
17 Mar	Celtic	H	47,312	1–1	McLaren
23 Mar	Falkirk	H	46,361	3–2	Gascoigne, Andersen (2)
30 Mar	Raith Rovers	A	9,300	4–2	McCoist (3, 1 pen), Durie (pen)
10 Apr	Hearts	A	15,350	0–2	
13 Apr	Partick Thistle	H	46,438	5–0	Andersen (3), McCall, Gough
20 Apr	Motherwell	A	13,128	3–1	McCall, Andersen, Gascoigne
28 Apr	Aberdeen	H	47,247	3–1	Gascoigne (3, 1 pen)
4 May	Kilmarnock	A	17,102	3–0	McCoist, Durie (2)

Position: Champions

PLAYER RECORDS (TOTAL)

Name	Apps	Subs	Goals
Goram	47		
Wright	16		
Robertson	38		4
Gough	4		25
McLaren	49		3
Petric	45	(1)	1
Steven	5	(2)	
Miller	28	(8)	6
McCall	31	(2)	4
McCoist	28	(9)	20
Durie	29	(9)	23
Durrant	8	(18)	
Salenko	18	(2)	8
Gascoigne	41	(1)	19
Laudrup	33		6
Moore	14	(2)	1
Murray	2	(7)	
Mikhailichenko	8	(7)	1
Cleland	29	(7)	4
Ferguson	22	(3)	6
Brown	14	(8)	
Scott	3		
Bollan	6	(1)	
Thomson	1	(1)	
McGinty	2		
McInnes	5	(1)	
Van Vossen	5	(4)	1
Andersen	6		6
Snelders	2		
Shields	1		
Hateley	4		2
Reid	1		
Own goals			4

Gordon Durie, the hat-trick hero of the Scottish Cup final. Rangers beat Hearts on 18 May 1996

SCOTTISH CUP

Date	Team	Venue	Att	Score	Scorer
3rd Round					
27 Jan	Keith	A	15,461	10–1	Ferguson (3), Cleland (3), Durie (pen), Robertson, Miller, Mikhailichenko
4th Round					
15 Feb	Clyde	A	5,722	4–1	Miller 2, Van Vossen, Gascoigne
Quarter-final					
9 Mar	Caledonian T	A	11,296	3–0	Thomson (o.g.), Gascoigne (2)
Semi-final					
7 Apr	Celtic	N	36,333	2–1	McCoist, Laudrup
Final					
18 May	Hearts	N	37,730	5–1	Laudrup (2), Durie (3)

LEAGUE CUP

Date	Team	Venue	Att	Score	Scorer
2nd Round					
19 Aug	Green Morton	H	3,396	3–0	McCoist, Hateley, Gascoigne
3rd Round					
30 Aug	Stirling Albion	H	39,540	3–2	Hateley, McCall, McCoist
Quarter-final					
19 Sept	Celtic	A	32,803	1–0	McCoist
Semi-final					
	Aberdeen	N	26,131	1–2	Salenko

EUROPEAN CUP

Date	Team	Venue	Att	Score	Scorer
1st Round					
9 Aug	Anorthosis	H	43,519	1–0	Durie
23 Aug	Anorthosis	A	9,500	0–0	
Champions' League Pool C					
13 Sept	Steaua Buch	A	26,000	0–1	
27 Sept	Borussia Dort	H	33,209	2–2	Gough, Ferguson
18 Oct	Juventus	A	50,000	1–4	Gough
1 Nov	Juventus	H	42,523	0–4	
22 Nov	Steaua Buch	H	30,882	1–1	Gascoigne
6 Dec	Borussia Dort	A	35,800	2–2	Laudrup, Durie

Season 1996–97

SCOTTISH CUP

Date	Team	Venue	Att	Score	Scorer
3rd Round					
25 Jan	St Johnstone	H	45,037	2–0	Andersen, Rozental
4th Round					
15 Feb	East Fife	H	41,064	3–0	Robertson, Steven, McCoist
Quarter-final					
6 Mar	Celtic	A	49,284	0–2	

LEAGUE CUP

Date	Team	Venue	Att	Score	Scorer
2nd Round					
14 Aug	Clydebank	A	6,376	3–0	Van Vossen(2), McCoist
3rd Round					
4 Sept	Ayr United	H	44,732	3–1	Albertz, Gascoigne, McInnes
Quarter-final					
17 Sept	Hibernian	H	45,104	4–0	Durie, Van Vossen (2), Albertz
Semi-final					
22 Oct	Dunfermline	N	16,791	6–1	Laudrup (2), McInnes, Andersen (2), Albertz
Final					
24 Nov	Hearts	N	48,559	4–3	McCoist (2), Gascoigne (2)

EUROPEAN CUP

Date	Team	Venue	Att	Score	Scorer
1st Round					
7 Aug	Alania	H	44,799	3–1	McInnes, McCoist, Petric Vladikavkaz
21 Aug	Alania	A	32,000	7–2	McCoist (3), Van Vossen, Vladikavkaz, Laudrup (2), Miller
Champions' League Group A					
11 Sept	Grasshoppers	A	20,030	0–3	
25 Sept	Auxerre	H	37,344	1–2	Gascoigne
16 Oct	Ajax	A	47,000	1–4	Durrant
30 Oct	Ajax	H	42,265	0–1	
20 Nov	Grasshoppers	H	34,192	2–1	McCoist (2)
4 Dec	Auxerre	A	21,300	1–2	Gough

Season 1996–97

PREMIER DIVISION

Date	Opponent	Venue	Att	Score	Scorers
10 Aug	Raith Rovers	H	46,221	1–0	Steven
17 Aug	Dunfermline	A	16,782	5–2	Van Vossen (2), McCoist (3, 1 pen)
24 Aug	Dundee Utd	H	48,285	1–0	Gascoigne
7 Sept	Motherwell	A	12,288	1–0	Gough
14 Sept	Hearts	H	47,240	3–0	Durie, Gascoigne, McCoist
21 Sept	Kilmarnock	A	14,812	4–1	Gascoigne (2, 1 pen), Van Vossen
28 Sept	Celtic	H	50,124	2–0	Gough, Gascoigne
12 Oct	Hibernian	A	12,436	1–2	Albertz
19 Oct	Aberdeen	H	50,076	2–2	Gascoigne, Laudrup (pen)
26 Oct	Motherwell	H	48,160	5–0	Laudrup (2), Gascoigne (3)
2 Nov	Raith Rovers	A	9,722	2–2	Van Vossen, McCoist
14 Nov	Celtic	A	50,009	1–0	Laudrup
1 Dec	Aberdeen	A	19,168	3–0	Robertson, Laudrup, Miller
7 Dec	Hibernian	H	48,053	4–3	Ferguson, McCoist (2), Laudrup
10 Dec	Dundee Utd	A	12,417	0–1	
14 Dec	Dunfermline	H	45,878	3–1	McCoist, Gough, Andersen
17 Dec	Kilmarnock	H	39,469	4–2	Andersen (3), Robertson
21 Dec	Hearts	A	15,139	4–1	Robertson, Laudrup, Albertz (pen) Gascoigne
26 Dec	Raith Rovers	H	48,322	4–0	Gough, Gascoigne, Albertz, McCoist
2 Jan	Celtic	H	50,019	3–1	Albertz, Andersen (2)
4 Jan	Hibernian	A	12,650	2–1	Andersen, Albertz (pen)
12 Jan	Aberdeen	H	47,509	4–0	Andersen (2), Albertz (pen), Laudrup
15 Jan	Kilmarnock	A	15,662	1–1	Gascoigne
18 Jan	Motherwell	A	13,166	3–1	Albertz, Laudrup, Gascoigne
1 Feb	Hearts	H	50,024	0–0	
8 Feb	Dunfermline	A	16,153	3–0	Durie, Albertz, Laudrup
23 Feb	Hibernian	H	47,618	3–1	Gough, Albertz, Laudrup
1 Mar	Aberdeen	A	16,331	2–2	Laudrup, Moore
12 Mar	Dundee Utd	H	49,192	0–2	
16 Mar	Celtic	A	49,733	1–0	Laudrup
22 Mar	Kilmarnock	H	50,036	1–2	Durie
5 Apr	Dunfermline	H	49,832	4–0	Albertz, Petric, Laudrup, Hateley
15 Apr	Raith Rovers	A	9,745	6–0	Petric, Durie (2), Robertson, Laudrup, McCoist
5 May	Motherwell	H	50,059	0–2	
7 May	Dundee Utd	A	12,180	1–0	Laudrup
10 May	Hearts	A	13,097	1–3	McInnes

Position: Champions

PLAYER RECORDS (TOTAL)

Name	Apps	Subs	Goals
Goram	38		
Steven	7	(3)	2
Albertz	46	(1)	13
Gough	41		6
Petric	35	(3)	3
Bjorklund	40		
Durie	20	(4)	7
McInnes	17	(16)	4
McCoist	20	(17)	20
McCall	13		
Laudrup	43		20
Durrant	7	(9)	1
Van Vossen	12	(14)	10
Miller	12	(9)	2
Cleland	45		
Gascoigne	31	(3)	17
Ferguson	24	(8)	1
Moore	31		1
Andersen	10	(15)	11
Boyack		(1)	
Snelders	7		
Shields	9	(1)	
Robertson	28	(2)	5
Wilson	3	(1)	
McLaren	12	(1)	
Rozental	1	(1)	1
Dibble	7		
Hateley	4		1
Fitzgerald		(1)	
Wright	2		
McGinty		(1)	
McKnight		(1)	

Paul Gascoigne and Ally McCoist celebrate winning the Scottish Coca-Cola Cup. They beat Hearts 4–3 in the Final on 18 November 1996

Index

Numbers in *italics* refer to pictures

A
Aberdeen 108–9, 112–13
Albertz, Jorg 78–9, *78*, *86*
Amoruso, Lorenzo 89
Andersen, Erik Bo 79–80, *79*

B
Baxter, Jim 12, *13*
Bjorklund, Joachim 80, *81*
Boli, Basile 81, *81*
Borussia Mönchengladbach 36
Brown, Bobby 11
Brown, John 54
Butcher, Terry 54–5, *55*

C
Celtic 8–9, 47, 50, 92–101
Centenary Cup Final 45
Cleland, Alex *43*
Club Deck Stand 21, 105
Collins, Gerry *14*
Cooper, David 12, 28
Copland Road Stand 104
Cox, Sammy 11

D
Dunfermline 113
Durie, Gordon *31*, *43*, *45*
Durrant, Ian *15*, *19*, *35*, 55–6, *56*
Dynamo Moscow 38

E
Elland Road, Leeds 40
European Champions' Cup 36–7, 40, 42
European Cup 35, 39
European Cup-Winners' Cup 36, 38, 105

F
Ferguson, Duncan 24, *25*
Ferguson, Ian 56–7, *57*
Forsyth, Tam 12

G
Gascoigne, Paul 30, *31*, 53, 57–8, *58*, 76, *111*, 112
Gattuso, Rino 88
Goram, Andy 20, 59, *59*
Gough, Richard 24, 29, 60, *60*, 100, 113
Govan Stand 107
Greig, John 13, 74, *74*

H
Hampden Park 24, 47, 49, 50, 52, 105
Hateley, Mark 18, *19*, *42*, 61, *61*, *98*, *101*, 108
Hearts 52, 110
Hibernian 49, 111–12
Holmes, David 13
Huistra, Pieter 18, 82, *82*

I
Ibrox Stadium 9, 36, 39, *106*
 architecture 102–3, *102–3*
 disaster 104
 reconstruction 105–6
Inter-Cities Fairs Cup 37

J
Johanson, Jonatan 88
Johnston, Maurice 16, *17*, *19*, 61–2, *62*, 96
Johnstone, Bobby 11
Johnstone, Derek 49
Juventus 39

K
Kerr, Stewart *101*
Knox, Archie *76*
Kuznetsov, Oleg 18–19, 82

L
Laudrup, Brian 27, *31*, *45*, 63, *63*
Lawrence, John 11
League Cup *see* Scottish League Cup
Leeds United 40
Leitch, Archibald 102–3
Lewis, Joe 106–7

M
McCall, Stuart 21, 64, *64*
McCoist, Ally *14*, 21, 28, 40, *41*, *51*, *57*, 64–5, *65*
McColl, Ian 11
McPhail, Bob 10
McStay, Paul *68*
Mikhailitchenko, Alexei 21, 83, *83*
Miller, Charlie 22
Morton, Alan 9, *9*, 10
Motherwell 110–11
Murray, David 15, *15*, *104*

N
Negri, Marco 91
Nou Camp, Barcelona 38

O
Old Firm matches 8–9, 92–101
Ormond, Willie 11

P
Petric, Gordon 84, *84*, 113
Porrini, Sergio *87*, 89
Premier Division 14–33, 95–7, 98–101, 108–13

R
Raith Rovers 110
Reilly, Lawrie 11
Robertson, David 21, 65–6, *66*
Rozental, Sebastian *32*, 87–8
Russell, Bobby 12

S
St Mirren 22
Salenko, Oleg 84–5
Scottish Cup 44–53
Scottish League Cup *13*, 44–53, 97
Scottish Premier Division 14–33, 95–7, 98–101, 108–13
Shaw, Jock 11
Shearer, Bobbie *48*
Smith, Andy *113*
Smith, Gordon 11, 13
Smith, Walter 20, *23*, *76*, 77, *77*
Souness, Graeme 13, *19*, 74, *75*, 76, 105
statistics 114–25
Stein, Colin 38
Stensaas, Stale *89*, 90–1
Steven, Trevor 21, 22, 66, *66*
Stevens, Gary 67, *67*
Struth, Bill 10, 71
Symon, Scot 11, 72

T
Thern, Jonas *90*, 91
Turnbull, Eddie 11

V
Vidmar, Tony 91
Vossen, Peter van 85, *85*

W
Waddell, Willie 12, 72–3, *93*, 104
Wallace, Jock 12, 50, 73–4, *73*
Walters, Mark 67–8, *68*
White, Chris *41*
White, Davy 72
Whyte, Derek *62*
Wilkins, Ray 68, *69*
Wilton, William 70–1
Woodburn, Willie 11
Wright, Steven 28

Y
Young, George 11, *11*